SR '77 0 5 8 2 4

796.91
Ar65b
*

DATE DUE			
SEP 6 - '77			
JAN 18 '78	Lin		
JAN 3 '78	Saw		
DEC 31 1992	Oly		
JAN 18 1993	main		

STUDENT ROOM

WITHDRAWN BY
HAMMOND PUBLIC LIBRARY

Hammond Public Library
Hammond, Ind.

Richard Arnold

Better Ice Skating

KAYE & WARD · LONDON
in association with Hicks, Smith & Sons
Australia and New Zealand

TO TRUDY AND DAVID

First published by
Kaye & Ward Ltd
21 New Street, London EC2M 4NT
1976

Copyright © Kaye & Ward Ltd 1976

All Rights Reserved. No part of this publication may be reproduced, stored in a retrieval system, or transmitted, in any form or by any means, electronic, mechanical, photocopying, recording or otherwise, without the prior permission of the copyright owner.

ISBN 0 7182 1442 0

Filmset in Monophoto Times by Computer Photoset Ltd
Printed in Great Britain by
Holmes McDougall Ltd, Edinburgh

Contents

	Acknowledgements	4
	Forewords	5
	Introduction	9
1	Let's Go Ice Skating!	11
2	The Great Adventure – First Steps	21
3	Elements of Figure Skating	30
4	Figure and Dance Skating	38
5	The Basic Eights	46
6	Turns	58
7	Simple Dances	65
8	More Advanced Dances	72
9	Free Skating	78
10	Outdoor Ice Skating	91
11	Now you Can Ice Skate . . .	93

Acknowledgements

I would like to express my thanks to the famous skaters who have been kind enough to write forewords to this book. Unfortunately, there is no room to tabulate all their successes in world, international and national events or the successes of their pupils. However, to my good friends Roy Lee and Anne Palmer, Former World Professional Ice Dance Champions, to David Clements, former British Men's Figure Skating Champion, British Olympic Representative, holder of several Ice Dance titles, and Television commentator on ice skating, and to David Hickinbottom, former British Ice Dance Champion I extend my gratitude, coupled with good wishes for their continued success in the future.

Thanks to John Neal, manager of the Westover Ice Rink, Bournemouth – home of former World Champions, for his kind words. John Neal has been associated with the production of ice shows for the best part of half a century and has made a magnificent contribution to this area of professional skating.

My thanks also to John Presland and the management of Queens Ice Club, London, for facilities to take photographs to illustrate this book, and thanks also to Diane Herman (Former British Junior Ice Dance Champion) and Christine Fry, teaching at Queen's, for their co-operation and enthusiasm. To Mitchel & King Skates Ltd, of Slough, Berkshire, my thanks for the provision of information about skates and photographs of different blades. Lastly, but not least, I am grateful to my old friend Andy Lock, skater and photographer, for many of the photographs taken for this book.

Saint Ives, Huntingdon, Cambridgeshire.　　　　　　　　　　　　RICHARD ARNOLD

Forewords

We are very pleased to be associated with this book by Dick Arnold. Quite often, after watching us training, or general public skating, Dick would say to us: "Some day I'll write a book about this – for the beginners." Well, Dick has done just that, and a good job he has made of it. As professional teachers of ice figure and dance skating we do appreciate the lack of something in writing dealing with the elements of skating. This book has been written simply, with the beginner in mind, and with its emphasis on acquisition of basic techniques and, above all, a good style, should be in every skater's library. We know Dick Arnold to have a lively approach to skating, and always to be eager to explore ways and means of helping the beginner.

ANNE PALMER
ROY LEE

Anne Palmer and Roy Lee (Mr & Mrs Roy Lee) are professional instructors with a long list of successes by their pupils in Ice Figure, Pair, and Dance Skating. They are former World Professional Champions in Ice Dancing and winners of the coveted "Gerald Palmer Trophy" awarded in connection with World Professional Ice Skating Championships. They are established teachers of long standing at the Sportsdrome, Richmond.

As a professional skating instructor, formerly a competition amateur, I have often felt that there is need for a simple primer on ice skating. I am, therefore, very pleased to welcome Dick Arnold's contribution *Better Ice Skating*, and delighted to have been invited to write a Foreword. Dick Arnold has been a skating friend of mine for some time and not only is he an enthusiastic skater but he is also a well-established author of many sporting books. This unique combination has resulted in a very valuable book to help the beginner to *understand* what ice skating is all about, as well as being of service to the enthusiast to better his or her performance on blades. Though conscious of the hard work involved in achieving proficiency in ice skating, Dick has never lost sight of its recreational value and its terrific "fun" element.

DAVID CLEMENTS

David Clements, Chairman of the International Professional Skating Association and currently an instructor at the Richmond Sportsdrome, formerly at Queen's Ice Club, is a former British Amateur Men's Champion in Figure Skating, a British Figure Skating representative in World, European and Olympic Championships and Competitions, and a former British Junior Ice Dance Champion. Holder of the N.S.A. Gold Medal for Figure Skating, he has trained many pupils to success, and is also a commentator on radio and television for ice skating events.

When Dick Arnold asked me if I would be kind enough to write a foreword to his book, I was very pleased. Dick Arnold has been around skating, both ice and rollers, for a long time, and his enthusiasm and love for the sport are very apparent to all who meet him.

With this book Dick has broken new ground, as it is intended primarily for the beginner. It is a good primer which will equally be of use to the coach. The emphasis is on a happy approach to skating and a concentration on acquisition of the basic elements, without which no skater can proceed further; above all the author concentrates on the necessity of skating in good style.

I, too, share Dick's enthusiasm for skating and I would like to congratulate him on this book and its companion volume *Better Roller Skating*, and wish him, and his readers, every success.

D. M. HICKINBOTTOM

David Hickinbottom, twice British Amateur Ice Dance Champion and winner in 1964 with Janet Sawbridge of the coveted N.S.A. European Trophy, has represented Great Britain in World and European championships. He has been a professional coach and has successfully trained British Roller Dance champions.

For many years Dick Arnold has been known to me as a friend and as a most enthusiastic skater with a particular interest in Ice Dancing. A very neat footed style and a wide knowledge of techniques has developed with the long period that Dick has been a devotee to the art of skating.

I am happy to have been asked to write a Foreword because as managing director and producer of the Bournemouth Ice Follies I represent the reason for which nowadays many study skating in a serious way and spend hard hours at practice, 'show skating.' It is the aim to become a show skater that keeps so many skaters hard at work and perhaps I am more fortunate than many as I have been able to do something that I enjoy doing – a hobby as well as a career. Dick Arnold, with his clear and concise book will undoubtedly help many, probably setting some of his readers on the road to show skating, or to teaching the lovely and rewarding art, or to further improve and develop their ability.

JOHN L. NEAL
Managing Director and Producer
Westover Ice Rink, Bournemouth.

John L. Neal commenced at the Westover Ice Rink in 1931, and was fortunate enough to be a colleague of the late Major H. G. Sharp. With Major Sharp and the late Phil Taylor John L. Neal was involved in the presentation of the first Ice Shows. With the exception of the War Years (1939-45) when the rink was closed and John was away with the Navy, he has served continuously at Westover. During that period the show skating business has expanded and now has ramifications all over the world. John has turned many leading amateur skaters into professionals, some of whom have become some of the most accomplished stars in the business, and 'discovered' names famous throughout the skating world. It should be noted, too, that Bournemouth has produced British and World Champions in Ice Skating as well as contributing to the professional show scene.

Introduction

Ice skating is tremendous fun! You only have to *visit* a rink to see how much everyone is enjoying themselves – the atmosphere is full of laughter punctuated by an occasional shriek of excitement. No matter whether you are an absolute beginner or a more advanced skater, this sport exercises a peculiar fascination. Ice skating presents you with a challenge, it gives you a sense of achievement as each new step or movement is learned and it is, above all, a very democratic sport. Families, old and young alike enjoy skating together and helping each other.

Another of the attractions of ice skating is that you can indulge any enthusiasm you may feel for a particular style of music, classical or pop, by skating movements that *express* the music. Also, you can dance alone, either practising the set steps of the officially-recognized dances or doing free dancing, without feeling self-conscious. Imagine anyone dancing alone in a ballroom!

Ice skating is an international sport and it features in the Winter Olympic Games. Most countries have their own national ice skating associations which regulate the sport as far as amateurs are concerned: they organize proficiency tests, and arrange competitive events and championships. These associations cover all aspects of the sport, ranging from speed skating to dancing, from figure skating to ice hockey, and they have made very valuable contributions to the high standard of skating witnessed today.

The aim of this book is to show you how to get the maximum enjoyment from skating and to help you start skating correctly. You have to learn the basic edges, body positions, carriage and so forth correctly, otherwise all your efforts will be wasted at a later stage. Skating should be an apparently effortless, graceful yet athletic, flowing movement over the ice, and this can only be achieved by mastering the four edges (outside, inside, forwards and backwards) and getting the necessary soft knee action. All skating, whether figures or dancing, whether jumping or turning, is based on these edges. Every skating movement requires a correct use of these edges; it is only too easy for a skater to throw himself or herself all over the rink, doing double or perhaps even triple jumps, spinning in many different ways, and look terrible! A less athletic skater, performing figures neatly and with style, with correct positioning of head and arms, perhaps travelling more slowly, though not performing the difficult movements of the first skater, will nevertheless not only look better but will also, in actual fact, be the better *skater*.

In the following pages I offer hints and tips that are the result of my own experience both as an amateur and as a professional coach. This book is not meant to supplant your instructor, but rather to help you understand what skating is all about, to help you supplement your coaching, and to help you to start skating properly before your first lesson.

A great deal of practice should be done *off* the rink, preferably in front of a mirror, so that you can see what you look like: to obtain the correct carriage, to check that your hands are carried naturally, and to see exactly what the position is that you are learning. By doing this you begin to know exactly how each position should *feel*. Each skating exercise should be supplemented by other physical exercises such as deep breathing, press-ups, etc. and smoking should be avoided.

Newcomers to skating who do not have an ice rink nearby generally skate for the first time on a frozen pond, where there are no rink barriers or bars to cling to. Because of this, they soon learn to get around by themselves. Whenever I teach a class of skaters, I absolutely forbid them to hold on to the barriers unless specifically instructed to do so (as in learning a Spread Eagle); I start my pupils from the T-position immediately, and on their second lesson they learn to stop and how to skate backwards. The T-position and other terms referred to in this introduction will be dealt with in detail in the following pages.

Now get your boots on and let's start skating!

1. Let's Go Ice Skating!

Once such an exciting suggestion is accepted, a whole new world opens up before you – a world in which you learn to glide over the surface of a rink with a peculiar sensation of freedom and exhilaration, almost like flying. It is also a world fraught with odd moments of fright, and the occasional bump and bruise.

THE ICE RINK

Some rinks are merely halls where skaters charge about the ice wildly, racing and playing, without any discipline whatever. These are dangerous places and have, in the past, given skating a bad name. Other rinks have special sessions for families, as well as dance skating and even speed skating. You would be wise to avoid the pop night rink sessions as these generally mean a disco with a disc jockey, loud music and lots of flashing lights. The 'teeny-boppers' who frequent these sessions are *not* skaters; such sessions do no good for skating, do not develop good ice skaters, and are merely a device to increase rink revenue by exploiting teenagers.

Try, therefore, to select an ice rink where skating competitions are held from time to time, where there is a professional coach or coaches in attendance, and where the music is suitable for skating to. Above all, try to go during a quiet session for your first venture. Winter school holidays and the periods immediately after the showing of skating championships on television often result in overcrowded rinks. As you will require room for your first ventures, try to avoid these times.

The rink is usually organized so that general skating goes round the ice rink in an anti-clockwise direction. No one is allowed to skate against this skating stream, because to do so would be dangerous. But, from time to time, an interval may be given to 'reverse' skating, in which the skaters travel round the rink in a clockwise direction. There may also be intervals for dancing, for fast skating, for ladies only, and for demonstrations. During these sessions you should only skate on the rink if you are capable of doing so without inconvenience to other skaters. For example, do not go on in a fast speed interval unless you are already competent to skate fast in safety, and are able to stop or swerve; do not go on in a dance interval unless you can perform the dance announced. Skating dances are set dances, rather like old-time or sequence dancing in the ballroom, and because skaters move swiftly it is essential that all the people participating skate the same steps, preferably at the same speed.

You can, however, learn a great deal by watching. Note how some skaters use their knees properly, how the expert carries his head, and how the dancers align their legs and feet. Observe what happens when a skater breaks the rules of good conduct by, perhaps, joining a dance sequence at the wrong moment or, inadvertently falling in the path of other skaters.

You are not allowed to smoke cigarettes or eat lollipops on the ice, as even a small piece of silver paper can lodge under a skate and bring the skater down with tremendous force. Dropping *anything* on to the rink surface is a very dangerous practice, particularly chewing-gum as it sticks to blades and causes accidents.

As you grow more confident, you may be tempted to skate faster and faster, until rebuked by a steward. Most rinks do not allow fast skating in the public sessions (except in specified intervals) because, with beginners and small children on the rink, unless a skater is in full control, there can be a nasty accident. Again, playing games like tag or tig and travelling together in chains or conga-files are banned on a well-run rink. Accidents, unfortunately, do happen to skaters and the practices I have described invariably result in someone getting hurt, usually not a participant.

CLOTHING

Everyone should avoid wearing headgear, long jewellery and baggy or very long jeans or trousers.

Until they become fairly proficient, girls would be well advised to wear trousers as they give some protection against grazes. A suitable blouse, jumper or jacket should also be worn. Slacks should not reach lower than the instep, otherwise they can get tangled either in the wearer's skates or in someone else's. After a few weeks, when a girl can move around with confidence, she may use more conventional skating attire: a small mini-skirt or a specially cut dress which flares out from the hipline. But 'way-out' colours and materials should not be used until the skater is really proficient, otherwise she will attract attention to herself *and* to her lack of skill. Under the skirt should be worn a matching pair of knickers or trunks, which can be sewn to the skirt, and these should be worn over the usual tights and briefs.

1. Many experienced skaters also wear slacks for practice periods.

Boys will find that slacks and a sweater or pullover are practical, though it is the fashion today to have special cat-suits or jump-suits made in stretch material. The beginner would be wiser, however, to leave these fashions to the very expert male skater.

In the early stages the beginner should not wear a wrist watch, firstly because it is easily damaged in a fall and secondly because pieces of broken glass left on the ice may cause injury to anyone who falls or puts a hand on them.

When skating in competitions, whether at rink, club or national level, and when skating proficiency tests, the candidate should wear suitable skating clothing: for the boys, slacks and a shirt or jumper, and for the girls a plain skating dress or leotard. However, some rinks do ban the wearing of leotards, while turning a blind eye to diminutive panties worn under a skating skirt – so please, girls, check first that leotards are acceptable to your rink management.

For outdoor skating you should not wear clothes that are too heavy, because you will warm up quite quickly, though a warm sweater should be kept handy to put on when you stop. Though the thought of wearing thick socks inside your boots may be appealing on a cold day, this is not in fact a wise thing to do: after the first few minutes skating, your feet become too tightly enclosed and your circulation is restricted, so that your feet get cold. Thin socks are adequate on even the coldest day.

If you get cold hands, especially skating outdoors, a pair of gloves is very useful. Do be careful though not to drop them on the ice for someone else to trip over. This can easily be avoided by sewing both of them on to a long piece of elastic or cord which goes up the inside of your sleeves and round the back of your neck.

HIRING ICE SKATES

Unless you have already skated on a frozen pond or lake in winter, you will make your debut at a rink, where skates are provided. Now, rink boots are not always very new! They have to withstand much punishment and ill-use, nevertheless they will enable you to skate without having to go to the expense of purchasing your own boots and blades. My advice is to use the rink equipment for several visits and not to buy your own until you know that you are going to take up the sport seriously. It is all too easy to become extremely enthusiastic and spend good money on equipment which, after a few weeks, you will not use any more.

It is customary to hand in your own boots or shoes in exchange for the hired ice skates. This does at least mean that you have the correct size to start with, though you may be a little dubious about wearing other peoples' footwear – especially footwear which had probably contained hundreds of different feet. So, the first precaution is taken before you go skating – make sure that your feet are well dusted with a good antiseptic foot powder, and that your stockings or socks are changed immediately after you have finished skating. Athlete's foot, an uncomfortable and itchy disease, is picked up very easily, particularly at swimming pools and from sharing boots. The simple precautions mentioned above help to resist it.

Do not wear thick socks or tights. The toes should not be tight and it is a good idea to specify skating boots about half a size less than your normal footwear. Rink boots are not easy to lace up properly, but you must be able to wiggle your toes inside them and they should be firm over the instep. Try tying a 'surgeon's knot' over the instep and then continue the lacing normally. Do not lace them too tight at the top as this will impede the circulation of your blood: it should be possible to insert two fingers into the top of the boot at the side.

BUYING BOOTS AND BLADES

These should not be purchased until you have decided that you are seriously going to take part in the sport. Fortunately for the skater who changes his or her mind, there is a ready market for second-hand boots and blades, especially amongst the childrens' sizes, but it is better to consider the matter carefully, as the outlay may be quite substantial.

When choosing boots, have them fitted at a shop which caters *specifically* for skaters. Most rinks have a skaters' shop which sells blades, boots, dresses, etc., and this should be the goal for the aspiring skate owner. The boots should be a snug fit and they should be bought *without* the blades fitted to them. The skating boot comes fairly high up the calf and when the boot is loosely laced up, the heel should be held securely. The boots should fit tightly, yet snugly, and allow for expansion of the leather, but, above everything else, the toe should not be tight. So, when purchasing, try on the boot wearing the socks or tights in which you are going to skate.

If you are a parent buying ice skates for a youngster, you will probably think, 'What an expense; he (or she) is going to grow out of them in no time'.

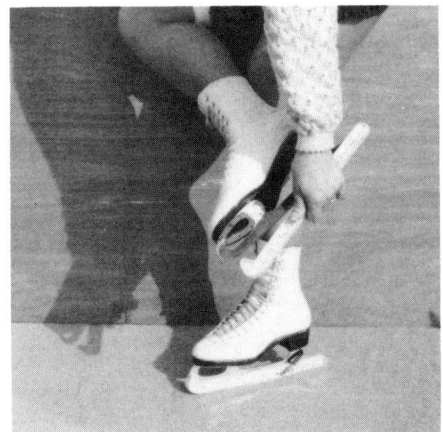

2. Make certain you remove your skate guards before starting to skate!

But childrens' boots do not get worn out by their first owner, they are outgrown. There is a ready market for them and many rinks have a notice-board which has 'for sale' and 'wanted' displayed on it.

Girls wear boots in white (or tan), whilst boys have black boots. When you buy boots and blades, you should also buy a pair of blade guards or protectors made of wood, leather or plastic which fit over the blades to guard them from damage. Two warnings, however: (a) always wipe the blades dry after skating before putting on the guards; and (b) remember to remove the guards before stepping on to the ice!

CHOOSING YOUR SKATES

Once you have got past the beginner stage and are able to perform elementary curves, figures and dance steps, you will need to consider the type of skates you are going to require. If you wish to become an expert figure skater, you will need skates of an advanced design. Incidentally most rented skates at rinks are figure blades. If you aspire to becoming an ice dancer, you will need a special type of blade. By the way, skaters do not talk about 'skates', they talk about 'blades'.

Naturally, the better the quality of the blade, the more expensive it is going to be, and you are advised to think carefully about the type of blade you are going to use and whether *you* will be good enough to do it justice.

Ice skates have developed into different types to meet different skating conditions. There are, of course, speed and hockey skates in addition to figure, free skating and dance blades.

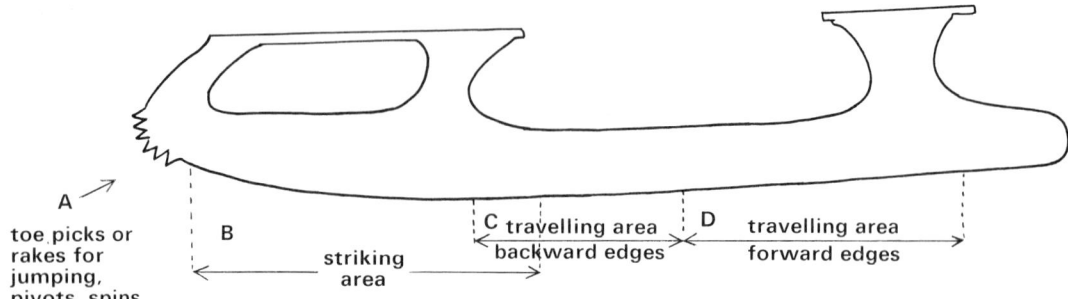

3. Analysis of an ice skate

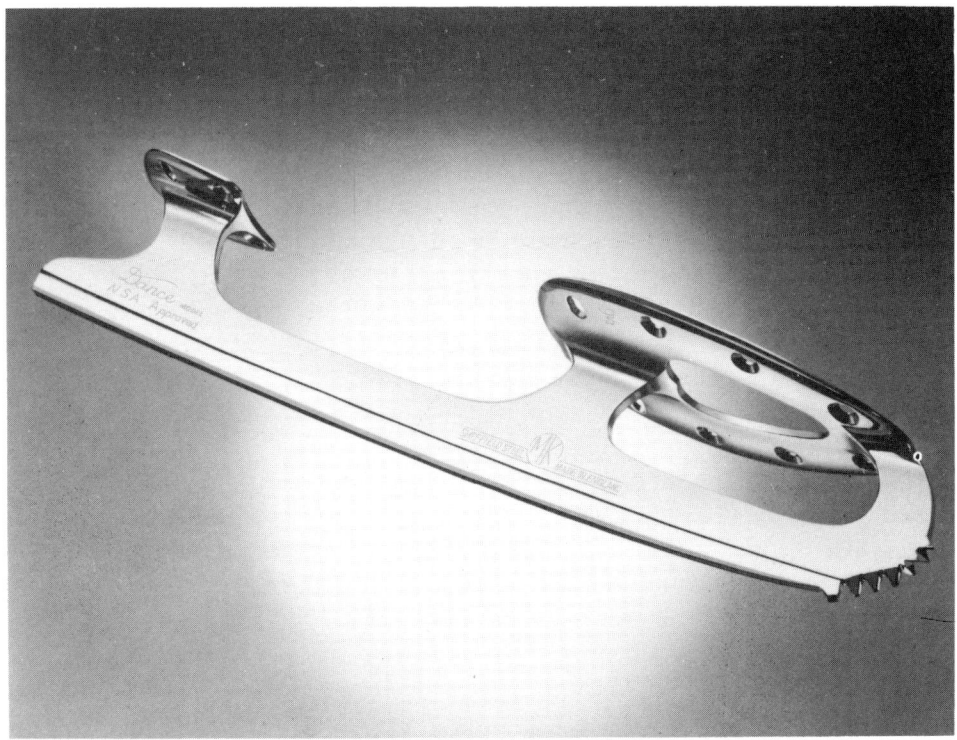

4. This skate has been designed for ice dancing. It has a reduced width skating edge which is narrower than the regular hockey blade! The tail of the blade is cut short, which allows close overlap of feet movements without the risk of tripping. The model shown, MK DANCE, has been chosen by world champions for many years.

The part of the skate which is most important is the blade. Its thickness, contour and toe pick design determine the effectiveness of a skater's performance. Speed blades have a very long, thin blade which is nearly flat. Hockey blades have to have some of the characteristics of the speed skate, but are shorter and a little thicker and have a contoured blade, which gives more manoeuvrability than the speed skate or racing blade. Figure skaters need maximum manoeuvrability and the blade of a figure skate has a very short ice contact with about 7 ft radius. To help the skater jump and spin the figure blade needs toe picks; on the other hand racing and hockey blades are smoothly curved at the toe.

THE TEST OF A GOOD BLADE

The steel must be 'through hardened' to an almost unbreakable temper. This hardness ensures a high polish and retention of edge. The high polish is essential for a fast-running blade, whilst a hard edge reduces the need for re-grinding.

In order for the skater to have maximum manoeuvrability and control over his movements, the blade must be straight and its contour must have a perfect radius or combination radius, with freedom from 'flats', which would prevent clean turns and figures. Special attention should be given to the toe picks. Each skater will have individual requirements for this refinement. Let's consider the different types of blades.

Figure Blades

In order to perform high-quality compulsory figure tracings, the hollow grinding must be shallow. This is necessary if 'double tracking' is to be minimized. The toe picks at the front of the skate must be set a little higher so that the clean ice tracing will not be spoiled by catching them.

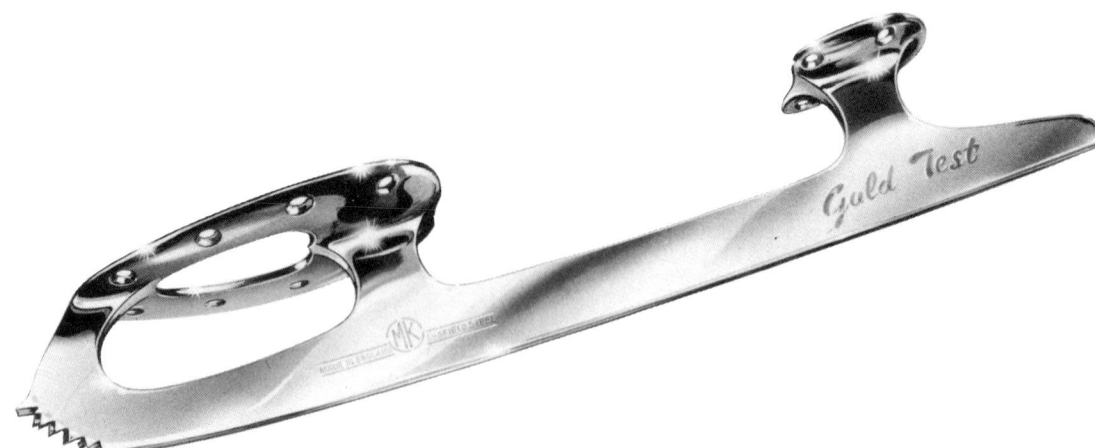

5. This blade, the MK GOLD TEST, is for the figure specialist. It has a shallow hollow grind which allows even flow throughout the entire tracing and, at the same time, helps the skater to avoid 'double tracking'. The toe-pick is arranged so that it does not project beyond the skating radius, and enables cleaner and deeper figure turns to be made. In backward skating there is no resistance to the water throw-off from a forward blade end.

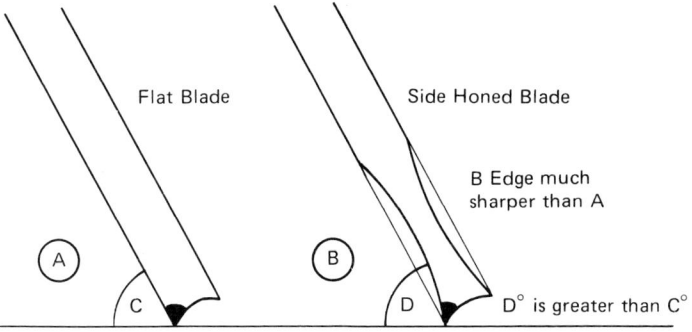

6. Difference between flat blade and side honed blade.

Free Skating Blades

These blades require an extra deep hollow grind in order to prevent slipping. Side honing of the blade is a feature which reduces weight and at the same time gives a better edge. Diagram 6 shows how side honing increases the ice grip at pronounced angles, where it is most needed. The toe picks are large, in combination form and include one large high pick giving the skater a really good ice grip when taking off in jumps.

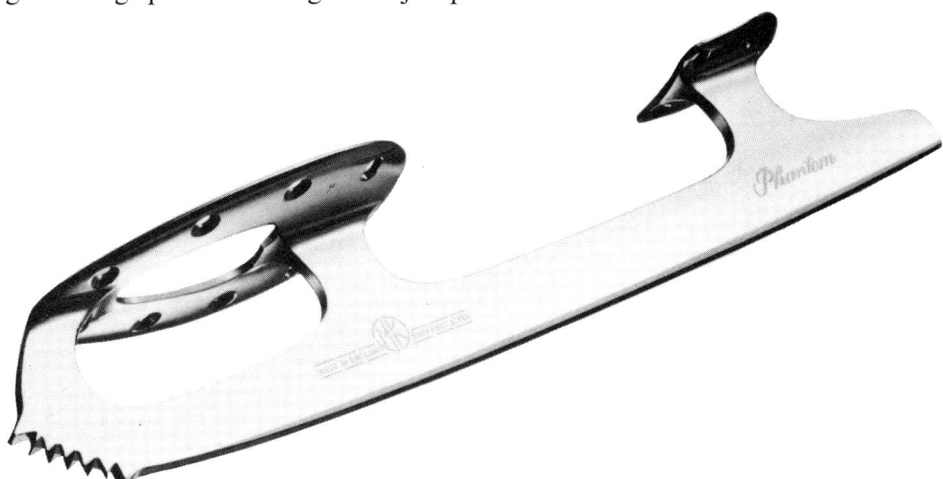

7. The skate shown is the MK PHANTOM, which is specifically a free skating blade. The toe-pick is well forward, ideal for jumping, and a feature of this skate is the long tail which helps with overall balance and performance.

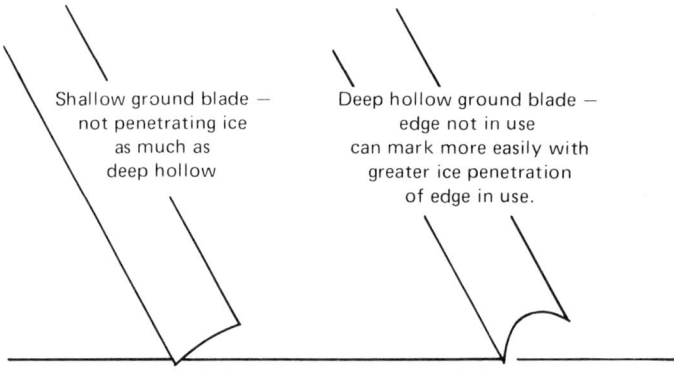

8. Shallow ground blade contrasted with deep hollow ground blade.

Dance Blades

These differ in that the blade heel is specially shortened to prevent skates colliding during fast and intricate footwork. The skating edge has a reduced width to give fast smooth running, with a minimum of effort.

Side Honed Blades

The term 'side honed' may puzzle you. Only one edge of a blade is used at a time and your body is always at an angle to the ice. For the same angle of body a larger angle of ice penetration is achieved with a side honed blade. Also, for the same depth of hollow grind a sharper inclusive angle is produced on the actual edge when the blade is side honed. The side honing operation is carried out in a straight longitudinal direction and does not follow the profile radius. The blade skating edge thus becomes tapered as the profile radius cuts further towards the centre of the side honing. This blade feature assists considerably in holding edges and in getting a good ice grip. As it is a slow and expensive operation, it is only found in the higher priced blades.

In the photographs of the skating blades, the dance, figure and free skating models shown are of very high quality such as used by leading amateur and professional skaters throughout the world.

2. The Great Adventure – First Steps

The most exciting moment in a skater's life is when he or she steps on to an ice rink for the first time. No matter how well you may have practised moving on skates *off* the rink, the moment you step on the ice all sorts of things happen. First of all the skaters whom you have been watching and admiring suddenly become fiends, travelling at high speed and apparently bent upon your destruction! They appear from nowhere, cutting in and out ahead of you, while the other beginners become dangerous obstacles who fall in your path or, even worse, clutch at you in a frantic effort to maintain their rapidly diminishing balance. Secondly, you suddenly become aware that you have no control over your feet and legs. The rink surface has become a place upon which you are absolutely helpless: you can go neither forwards nor backwards, you cannot start to move and, if you do, you cannot stop . . ! Fortunately the problem of maintaining your balance gradually overcomes your apprehension about the other skaters, and the feeling of helplessness soon turns to one of exhilaration as you take your steps.

When you stand up for the first time, the ice skates will feel thin beneath you and there will be a tendency for your ankles to drop over, though you will be able to stand erect on the blades and move your ankles forwards or backwards. As you walk towards the ice, your confidence will return, but, a word of caution: you have to step *down* on to the ice on most rinks, through an opening in the barrier. The transition from walking on matting or rubber flooring to a slippery ice surface and stepping downwards at the same time is the most perilous moment in a skater's career!

Carefully stand with both feet together parallel to the barrier, and hold the barrier with your right hand. Keep all your weight evenly distributed over both feet. Make sure you are not going to step into the path of another skater, then carefully move your left foot sideways and place it firmly on to the ice. Stand erect and do not lean in any direction. Still holding on to the barrier, transfer your weight on to your left foot on the ice. Lift your right foot and put it down alongside the one on the ice and then transfer your weight so that it is evenly spread over both feet.

The floundering and wobbling, the thrashing of arms and perhaps even the falls which follow may seem interminable, but within a few minutes you will be making your way round the rink. The first lap will seem to take hours, but each lap will become easier.

With the confidence you have found from your first efforts on the rink, you are ready to start making your first skating 'stroke'.

T-POSITION AND SKATING STROKE

Stand upright and perfectly still. Your feet should be in a T-position, that is your left foot should be behind your right foot, with your right heel in the instep of your left foot at right-angles. Your knees should be bent. Still standing stationary and erect, with your weight evenly distributed over both feet, gradually transfer your weight to your left leg. In order to push yourself

9, 10. Commence the strokes from the T-position. Push-off from the side of your skate, straighten your rear leg and bend your skating leg. Glide away with the push-off leg extended behind you. The skating knee is bent; the extended push-off leg slightly bent with the knee turned out, and the foot turned out and pointed nicely.

forward into the stroke, it is necessary to anchor your pushing skate, in this instance the left one, against the ice. You do this by turning your left ankle inwards, so that the edge of the blade will give a firm base for you to thrust against. Now bend both knees *deeply*.

Keep your right foot directly under your body. Now straighten your left knee (rear leg) and transfer your weight to your right leg, keeping your right knee deeply bent.

Providing you have done this properly, your straightened left leg will start you moving over the ice on your right skate!

Leave your left leg behind, with the blade only an inch or so above the ice, and slowly bring your left arm forward to help you balance. Hold the glide forward as long as you can, with your body held perfectly upright.

You will thus have completed a skating stroke, and the next one to follow is done by bringing your left foot to the T-position against your right foot, heel to instep, and repeating the action: bend both knees, then straighten your right leg, which will propel you over the ice on your left skate.

Two strokes are enough to start with. Then stop and start again from standstill until you can *feel* the balance of each skate. When travelling forwards your weight should be to the rear of the skate blade and the push-off by the propelling foot must be done by using the flat of the whole skate blade. Do not use your toe rakes or toe picks to push off with.

Now try to travel a little further with each stroke, and you will soon be skating properly.

11, 12. The dreadful effects of toe-picking. Besides being incorrect it is ugly and results in terrible body postures. In skating circles toe-picking is anathema. Toe picks may, within reason, be used for running steps and in some spins and jumps.

HOW TO STOP!

Having learned to move forward, the next thing to learn is how to stop. In most ice skating tests organized by national skating associations the first elementary tests are (a) to skate across the rink without falling down *and* (b) to stop when skating forward at a reasonable speed.

Various directions may be given for stopping when skating forward, but they all have this in common: the use of the toe picks or rakes must be avoided.

When learning to stop, it is advisable to glide forward on both feet, with your weight evenly distributed between them. Keeping your feet about a foot apart, you should then turn your head to one side, generally to the left, and at the same time turn in the same direction on a sharp curve. As the curve commences, the foot which comes forward should then be turned even more sharply and your weight kept well back. The front skate will then bite against the ice with the side of the blade and bring you to a halt.

On the other hand it is possible to stop by swinging your hips sharply to one side, with both feet again parallel and about a foot apart, bringing your weight well back. Both skates will then slide over the ice to stop you.

Another method is to select the foot on which you are skating best, then allow the other foot to glide to the rear, about a foot behind the skating foot. Gently lower your free foot on to the ice and, by gradually increasing pressure on the blade, allow it to scrape across the ice and gently bring you to a standstill. This last method does, however, require considerably more 'braking distance' than the other two methods described.

13. Stopping by letting the front skate curve round and bite into the ice.

14. You can stop by swinging the hips to one side and with both feet parallel slide them sideways to direction of travel.

FALLING OVER

By this time you will have tumbled at least once – probably lots of times. When a fall is imminent, try to relax and allow yourself to collapse on to the ice. If you are tense or rigid, you are much more likely to injure or bruise yourself. Do not try to break a fall by putting a hand out; the ice can give you a 'burn', and it is possible to break a wrist by doing this. Also if your fingers are spread out on the ice, there is the possibility that someone will skate over your hand or fingers and cut you badly.

Let yourself go in a fall whenever you have the time to realize that you cannot avoid it. Then, in order to get up again, do not try to climb up another skater or the barrier! Get into a position in which you are kneeling on one foot with the other foot squarely on the ice. Now, place all your weight on the skate on the ice, anchoring yourself by means of the toe pick if you wish, and gently raise yourself. The moment you are able to stand up, put your feet into the T-position so that you are ready to skate again. Do not try to crawl across the rink to reach the barrier, as this usually results in disaster!

CURVES AND RUNS

So far you have gone round the rink in a series of short glides and shuffles, but skating really consists of progression by means of a series of curves, not straight lines, and now is the time to consider what you are doing. If you look at your skates, you will notice that there is a hollow down the centre of the blade; this is termed *hollow grinding* or *hollow ground*. The two sharp sides of the hollow are called the *edges* of the skate. The edge of the skate on the inside of the foot, the same side as the big toe, is called the *inside* edge, while the edge of the skate on the outside of the foot, on same side as the little toe, is called the *outside* edge.

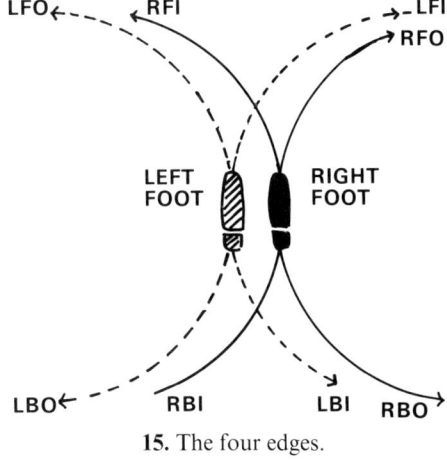

15. The four edges.

When skating curves, as we shall see presently, the skater does not skate on the entire surface of the blade, i.e. on both edges at once, but on one or other of the two edges. If you were to skate on both edges at once, you would not be skating an edge at all but on the *flat* of the skate. You must learn these terms now, as all skating is based on these edges.

Look again at your skates. The blades are not straight from toe to heel, but are set on a slight curve. This curve is called the *radius* of the skate – usually figure skates are on a seven foot radius. The use of the curved skate allows the skater to transfer his weight from forwards to backwards along the skate to suit the skating conditions; for example, skating forwards is done with the weight on the back portion of the skate, and the front of the skate is clear of the ice. Certain turns are performed over different parts of the blade, and the toe picks are used for jumping, certain spins, and running steps.

A curve on one foot skating forward to the left may be either an outside forward edge skated on the left foot or an inside forward edge skated on the right foot. Likewise, identical curves skated backwards may be backward inside or backward outside edges. This may sound confusing, but in reality it is remarkably simple.

In figure, dance and pair skating there are only four edges – no more. These are inside and outside, forwards and backwards. Convention has decreed a certain identification code for these edges, which is used internationally. The capital letter R indicates a right-footed edge or figure; the capital letter L indicates a left-footed edge or figure. The small letter f indicates forwards, b indicates backwards, i indicates inside edge and o indicates outside edge. Thus: Rfo means an outside edge skated forwards on the right foot; Lbi means an inside back edge skated on the left foot. Certain turns – which we will learn about later – are identified by capital letters, but they do not concern us at this stage.

The whole foundation of figure, dance and pair skating is dependent upon these four basic edges. With the exception of certain movements and spins, all skating movements are a combination of these edges in one form or another and *a skater is only as good as the edges he skates.* For example, the take off and landing of even the most difficult jump must be executed from edge to edge (except in toe jumps) and special attention is paid by judges in tests and competitions as to whether or not a spring is made from a true edge to a clean landing on a true edge. Thus, if you can realize that even the most advanced figure is a sequence of edges (requiring the appropriate body, arms, leg, head and foot positions), you are well on the way to becoming a proficient skater.

When you were learning to stop by coasting along on parallel skates and curving to one side, you were beginning to find control over directional skating, but you were not skating an edge, as you were running on the flat of the blades. Let us try, therefore, a simple curve on the outside edge of the skate.

Start by making a series of forward strokes from the T-position push-off. As you glide on your left foot, leaving your right foot behind you with the toe 2-3 inches above the ice, keep your left knee bent. Now lean to the left. At this point your body must be in an *unbroken* line from the crown of your head to your foot – no leaning from the waist or hips! You will feel the edge as your skate bites into the ice and you will start a curve to the left. Hold this as long as you can, then gently bring your right foot forward until it touches your left foot; bend both knees strongly and turn the toe of your right foot out to an angle of about 45°. Now straighten your left leg and, at the same time, step on to your right skate, and start leaning to the right. The bring your left foot forward until it touches your right foot and go through the procedure again, this time stroking to the left.

You are now stroking and skating short curves or edges between each push-off or stroke. Try to lengthen each glide between strokes, counting 1-2-3-4, etc. as you glide on each foot.

CROSS-OVERS

As you skate round the rink, you will find that, whereas with your first short steps you were able to negotiate the curve at each end, it becomes increasingly difficult to get round with longer curves and strokes – the cross-over helps you overcome this problem. However, there is more to a cross-over than just using it to get round the end curve of a rink: it is a very attractive movement, especially for pair skaters.

Let us commence with a cross-over to the left, which is the easiest to learn, because it follows the natural progression round the rink in an anti-clockwise direction. Commence by skating on a left forward outside stroke, with your right foot extended behind. Now bring your right foot forward close to your left foot but, instead of stopping it beside your left foot, continue bringing it

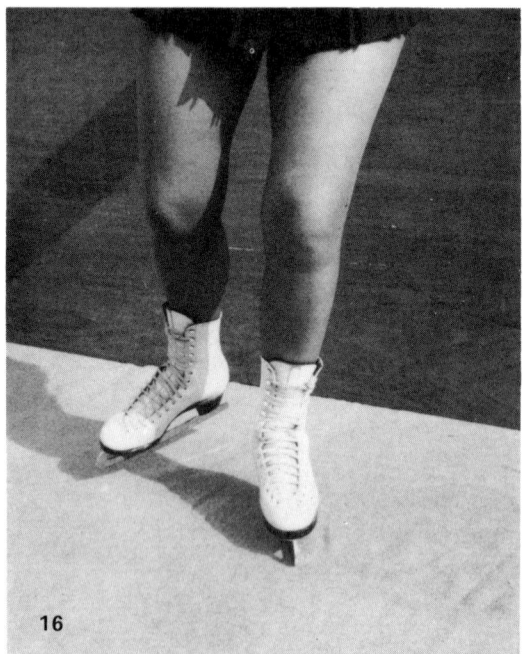 

direction of skating⟶

16-19. For the forward cross-over, skating in an anti-clockwise direction, bring the trailing right foot ahead of the skating foot and across the skating line. The right foot is then placed on the ice on the inside of the curve and the weight taken on it. The left foot is then taken forward and the stroke taken normally from the right foot.

forward until it has passed your left foot. You are now leaning, with bent left knee, on to a left outside edge. Your right arm and shoulder should be forward, and your left arm and shoulder back. In other words, you are in a strong contra-body position, that is an exaggerated walking position. Now, cross your right foot wide over in front of your left skate into the inside of the curve. As your right foot is placed on the ice it should take up an inside edge and be absolutely parallel to your left foot. As you step over, your weight should be immediately transferred to your right skate. Your left skate will, virtually of its own accord, slide off the ice with the left leg in an extended position. Your left knee should be straight, and your left foot should be pointing, still in a crossed-under position, to the outside of the circle. Now, bring your left

18

19

foot forward and stroke on to a normal left outside edge. You have thus completed the cross-over.

It is important that the skating knee should always be bent – it is impossible to execute a cross-over with straight legs. You must not push during the cross-over – the push is done on to the inside leg – the cross-over is a glide using the impetus of the original stroke. Remember that the knee of the leg which has been crossed should be absolutely straight and a smooth action must be striven for. Each cross-over means that you are skating alternatively an outside forward edge on the left foot and an inside forward edge on the right foot.

When you feel confident about cross-overs to the left, start circling to the right, i.e. in a reverse direction, and cross the left foot over the right, until you can do cross-overs each way smoothly, neatly and confidently.

3. Elements of Figure Skating

Figure skating consists of solo skating by individual skaters and of skating in pairs (girl and boy), termed 'pair skating'. In professional and show skating, figure skating can be performed by a combination of several skaters, e.g. a trio, two people of the same sex, or by what are termed 'line' skaters in chorus or formations.

Amateur skating is controlled by the national ice skating associations of each country, affiliated to an international body, and figure skating is composed of what are called 'school' or 'compulsory' figures for solo skaters, plus what are termed 'compulsory programmes', that is a short programme with compulsory moves, for free skating and pair skating. Free skating consists of a programme of different skating movements – jumps, spins, edges and linking steps – skated in harmony with suitable music. In international and national competitions for amateurs, certain jumps and spins are specified to be included in the 'compulsory' short programmes for free skating and pair skating.

The skating must be carried out in accordance with basic rules of correct carriage, motion and flow. (There is a special style of skating, termed the English Style, which differs from the International Style in that compulsory figures, skating movements and turns are on a different schedule and there is not the same freedom of arm and leg movement; it is chiefly confined to a few enthusiasts in England.) The rules of style which follow are applicable to what is called the International Style of Figure Skating.

When learning basic figures, you must at all times strive to conform to the rules of good form, which are briefly:

1. There should be no stiffness of your body or limbs.
2. The upper part of your body should be erect and not bent forwards or to either side at the hips.
3. Your arms must not be held too high, and must be carried gracefully and easily to assist movement.
4. Your hands should not be carried above the waist. Indeed, one cannot stress this point often enough: stiff, rigid fingers and clenched fists are anathema; the hands should be carried with palms downwards and held naturally and easily.
5. Stiff, tense, or exaggerated postures have to be avoided. Thus, your skating leg should have a slightly bent knee and your free leg, which should also be slightly bent at the knee, should be carried over the tracing line.
6. The toe of your free foot should point downwards and outwards, and should be carried neither too high off the ice, nor too close to your skating foot.
7. Your head must be held in a relaxed and natural upright position.
8. You should raise and lower your body by bending the knee of your skating leg. Abrupt and jerky movements must be avoided, and the whole impression should be of a smooth, effortless flow, carried out at a reasonable speed.

FIGURE SKATING TERMS

In the above rules of good carriage for figure skating we have referred to 'tracing leg', 'free leg', etc. Such terms need not confuse the novice; in photographs 20 and 21 you will see a skater executing right forward inside and outside, edges, with various terms identified.

FIGURE SKATING POSITIONS

With minor alterations to head position depending on whether you are going forwards or backwards, there are basically only four positions to be adopted when you are executing school figures (here we are referring to the edges and not to turns). These positions (A, B, C and D) are shown in photographs 22-25.

The head position will vary, because you have to look in the direction in which you are skating, but otherwise these are the basic positions. As you

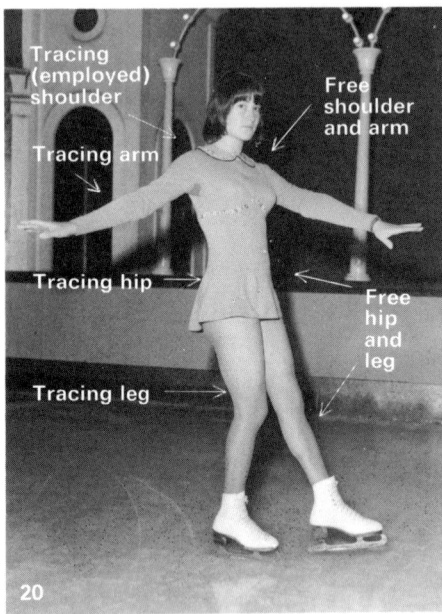

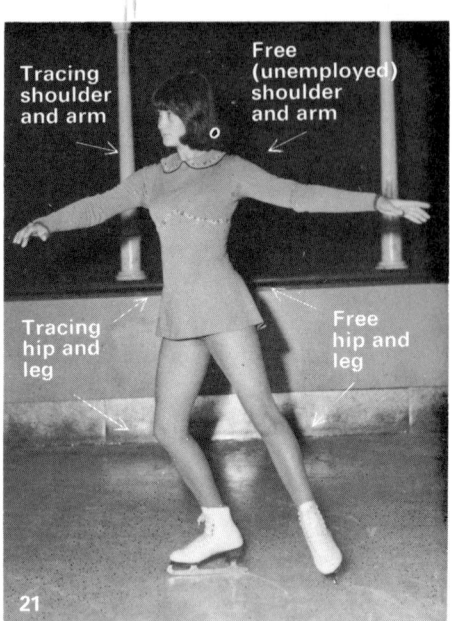

20, 21. In these two photographs the terms skating or tracing side and the free side are defined. On the left the skater is on a left forward inside edge, in the right hand picture on a right forward outside edge.

change from one position to another during the figure, there are of course intermediate positions to enable you to start the second half of the figure in the correct way.

22. Position A – Tracing or employed shoulder and arm leading; free leg, shoulder, arm, and hip held back.

23. Position B – Tracing shoulder and arm back; free leg, shoulder, arm and hip forward.

SCHOOL OR COMPULSORY FIGURES

Apart from elementary and preliminary tests organized by the various national skating associations, school or 'compulsory' figures are skated over two or three circles, which join each other apart from a very small break in their continuity due to the skater changing from one skating foot to the other. The circles are all approximately of the same diameter.

The nomenclature of figures should be learned, for example, the circles (whether in two- or three-circle form) must be placed centrally over what are termed 'long' and 'transverse' (or 'short') axes (see diagrams 26 and 27). It is essential that you observe the placing of the figure so as to maintain both axes.

The skater has to indicate the long axis which he or she is going to use *before* the figure is skated. In competitions and championships the skater is not allowed to use the long axis provided by a figure previously skated, nor may he use ice markings (e.g. hockey or curling rings or lines) or mark the ice by scratching it with his skate in order to identify the start, the axes, or the placement of turns.

24. Position C – Tracing shoulder and arm, and free leg and hip back; free shoulder and arm forward.

25. Position D – Tracing shoulder and arm forward; free leg and hip forward; free shoulder and arm back.

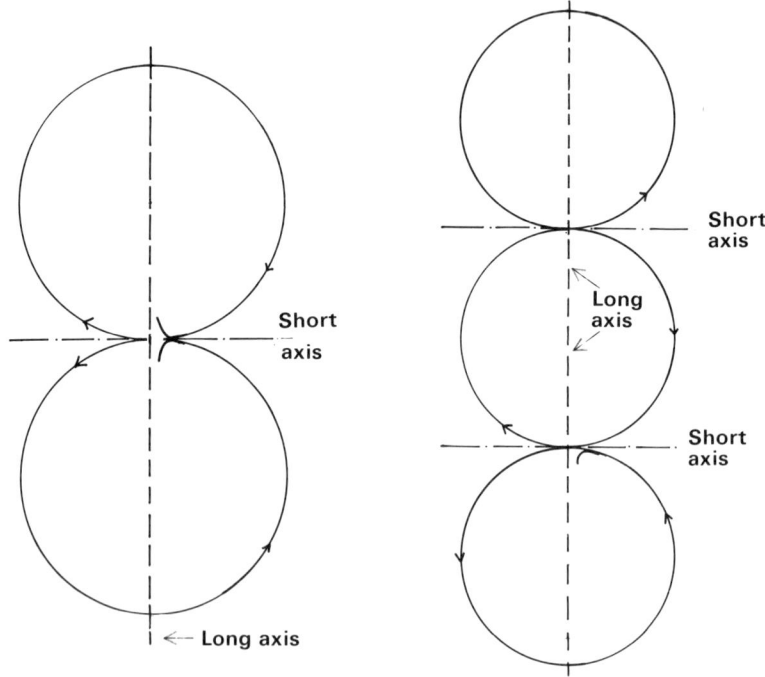

26. A two-lobe figure.   **27.** A three-lobe figure.

PRELIMINARY TESTS

Most associations which have elementary and preliminary proficiency tests do not require you to skate the figures over circles but allow you to lay down the figures on 'curves', 'rolls' or 'in field'. The strict rules applying to starting from rest, i.e. not employing preliminary steps to obtain impetus, do *not* apply to these tests. However, the standards insist that the 'curves' or 'rolls' should be sufficiently long to enable judges to see that the candidate has good carriage and deportment, can skate with reasonable speed, and has control over his or her edges. The lines skated must be free of wobbles.

Each figure which is started on one foot must commence in an identical body position on the other. This means a change of body position whilst skating the curves or complete circles, so that the correct position is assumed for the take-off on completion of the finishing curve. At this stage, however, we will concentrate on the preliminary or elementary rolls or curves.

ROLLS OR CURVES

Outside forward: These rolls are skated first on one foot and then on the other, along the same long axis. Take up your usual T-position so that the toe of your right foot is along the line of the transverse axis. Your back will be to the centre of the circle you are going to skate. You will be sideways to the direction of travel, i.e. your skating shoulder and hip will be leading, while your free hip and shoulder will be directly behind. This is Position A. Turn your head over your skating shoulder. Keep this position when you have taken your stroke by pressing your free hip, leg and shoulder back, and leaning your whole body to the right. Keep your free foot turned out and pointed directly over the line made by your tracing foot. Your free shoulder must be approximately level with your skating shoulder or a fractional amount lower. *Keep your hips level.* You should feel yourself exerting a downward pressure on the free hip – this will maintain the correct skating position and correct weight distribution over your skate.

Inside forward: Commence with the T-position, but this time face your body squarely over your right foot. This figure uses a 'contra-body' position and the left or free shoulder and arm must be held forward, whilst you press the tracing or right shoulder and arm back. After you have made your stroke, keep your hips forward and your shoulders at right-angles to the line of your skating foot. Keep your shoulders level. Your free leg must be carried inside the circle or curve, quite close to your skating leg, with the heel of your free foot over the tracing line. Look over your free shoulder (the left shoulder) at the centre of the curve you are making.

The above two rolls or curves should be practised, stopping between rolls, until you feel completely at ease and happy about them. A certain amount of practice before a mirror is necessary to find out not only how the body and arm positions look but also how they *feel*, so that they can be assumed naturally and easily.

SKATING BACKWARDS

Oddly enough, most skaters find skating backwards easier than skating forwards! Skating backwards is not difficult to learn, probably because by the time a skater comes to learn to skate backwards he or she is already fairly proficient at skating forwards and has gained a sense of balance.

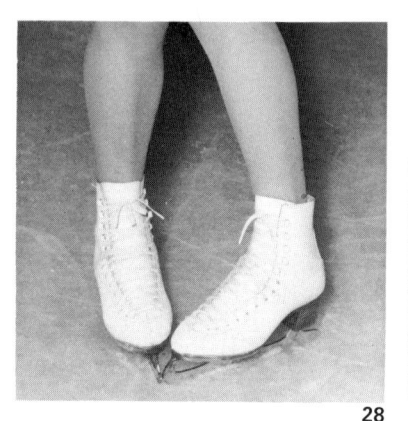

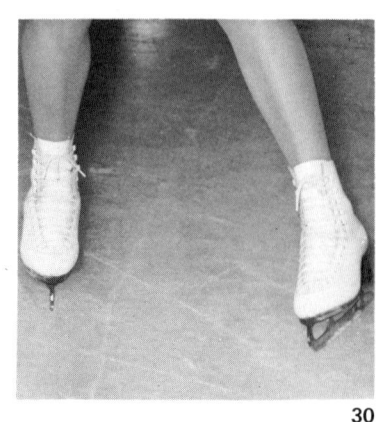

28-30. Commence skating backwards with bent knees and toes turned in, then transfer weight from foot to foot, leaving your pushing foot as a free foot in front of you. The stroking is from inside edge to inside edge.

When skating forwards, you will have found that the feet are positioned so that the toes are turned out and the stroke is made by pushing with the whole of one skate from the heel of the other – the reverse applies to skating backwards. Logically enough, if your toes have to be turned out when skating forwards, then your heels have to be turned out when skating backwards.

Stand up, with your toes turned in towards each other and your knees bent. Now, transfering your weight on to one foot, lift the other completely off the rink and carry it backwards a few inches, placing it fair and square, with the toe still pointing forwards. This foot should only be carried back to about mid-way along the skating foot. So far so good. Now, transfer your weight to the skate just placed on the rink, lift the other foot, toe still turned in, and repeat the procedure. Keep standing erect, with your head up. You will find that you are able to walk backwards like this quite confidently.

After you have done this several times, as you lift one foot, press the skating foot (the one on the ice) and push against the other foot as it is placed in position. You will find yourself skating on an inside edge backwards. Hold this position as long as you can, counting up to 3 between strokes.

Practise this for a while, then start again in the following manner.

Stand up perfectly erect, with knees bent, then (with toes turned in) transfer all your weight on to your right leg and at the same time slide your left skate off the rink surface in front of you. Point your left toe and straighten the knee of your left leg. This should bring your left foot off the rink and in line with the toe of your right skate (photograph 25). But do not lift your free foot too high! Now bring your left foot back until it is parallel with your right foot, but do not put it down on the rink just yet. Straighten your right knee and at the same time drop your free foot on to the surface directly beneath you and shift your weight on to it. Your right skate should lift off the rink in front of you and slightly to the right side. You will now be gliding back on your left foot, on the inside edge. Now lean your body on the next stroke to the side so that you will automatically stroke on to the outside edge. The mechanics are simple: *you skate on the outside edge, but you push off from the inside edge*. Your weight must be transfered from one foot to the other when they are close together and immediately under the body. The free leg must be straight, while the glide is on a bent leg.

STOPPING BACKWARDS

When you are skating backwards and wish to stop, gradually bring your weight forwards so that your toe picks brake you. Alternatively, you can carry your free skate backwards as far as possible then place it on the ice at right-angles to your skating foot. The blade will anchor itself and, by keeping your weight forwards and gradually bringing your skating foot up to the anchored free foot, you will stop. Another method is to skate backwards, bring both skates parallel but apart, then swing your hips to one side and turn your skates sharply at the same time. This is the counterpart of forward stopping.

TURNS FROM FORWARDS TO BACKWARDS

Simple turns from forwards to backwards are made on both feet. Bring your feet parallel to each other, about 9 inches apart. Now gradually bring your shoulders round in the direction in which you wish to turn, e.g. if you wish to turn to the left, in an anti-clockwise direction, pull your left shoulder back and bring your right shoulder and arm forwards. Now quickly shift your weight from the back part of the blades to the part of the blades which is just forward of centre. Bring your right hip forward under your right shoulder and you will automatically turn on both skates at once into a backwards position. Do not lean forwards at all, but maintain an erect position. Keep your body at right angles to the skates when you have turned backwards.

4. Figure and Dance Skating

Most beginners imagine, quite wrongly, that free skating and dance skating are for experts only. They are under the impression, again quite wrongly, that one is virtually compelled to skate for proficiency tests. This impression is probably gained because most dancing on skates is limited to the schedule of dances approved by the National Association, and may be either the subject of tests or be used as compulsory dances in international competitions and championships.

This situation is often very discouraging to the keen skater. He or she probably wishes to be able to turn from backwards to forwards and vice versa, to skate simple dance steps, and to be able to skate solo to music (free skating) without wishing to pass any national proficiency tests. In other words, there are today untold thousands of skaters who could improve their standards and participate in *social* skating, including dancing, if more imagination were used by including simple non-official dances in public skating sessions.

We hope that the notes which follow will enable the average enthusiast to skate safely and enjoy certain basic dances, and, in a later chapter, you will be introduced to dances which do not appear in the international schedule, but which nevertheless *require skating skill* and are very enjoyable to perform.

OPEN CHASSÉ

In this step you put your free foot on to the rink alongside your skating foot and, as both feet are momentarily together on the ice, the original skating foot

31, 32. You put your free foot on the ice alongside your skating foot, lift your original skating foot momentarily and then replace it, and resume the skating position. Read the photos from right to left, and then back again, from left to right.

is lifted, the free foot becomes the skating foot for a moment, then the original skating foot is replaced alongside and the original skating position is assumed.

This may sound complicated, so try this in practice first without skates. Stand on both feet. Step forward (without stroking) on to your left foot – this would mean, if you were on skates, that your left foot would be the skating foot. Hold your right leg and foot behind as if you had just taken a stroke. Now bring your right foot forward parallel to your left foot. Place it on the ground. Do not pass your left foot with your right foot. Lift your left foot clear of the floor, not too high, and stand on your right foot for a second. Then quickly replace your left foot alongside your right foot, and lift your right leg back in the free leg position of a stroke.

The chassé has thus been completed to the left. Now bring your right foot forward into the T-position and strike from left to right foot, and repeat the chassé movement, this time to the right.

Now you can practise this with your skates on, but remember: as one foot goes down beside the other, the original skating foot, is lifted and then replaced.

A good free leg and a good bent skating knee are essential if a chassé is to be performed properly. One sometimes sees skaters bringing their free leg alongside their skating foot and then pushing forward on to the skating foot – this is *not* a chassé. Incidentally, it is a very bad habit to lift only the rear of the

33, 34. In a crossed chassé the free foot is crossed *behind* the skating foot, which is then lifted and placed on the ice ahead of and to the side of the crossed behind foot. Read the photos from right (34) to left (33) and back to right again.

skate instead of the whole of it, and there is often a tendency to lift the foot too high. The skate should merely be lifted enough to ensure that it is clear of the ice.

You should practise this chassé both forwards and backwards – the movements are the same in either direction and are easy to learn.

CROSSED CHASSÉ

This is a little more difficult, but, providing you have mastered your edges and forward cross-overs, a crossed chassé is fairly quickly learned. Practise a forward crossed chassé without skates first of all.

Stand on your left foot in a skating position, with your right foot and leg stretched behind in a free position. Now, keeping your weight over your left foot, bring your right foot behind your left foot so that your feet are in a crossed position. Lift your left foot from in front of your right foot and place it on the ground ahead and to the side of your right foot so that your left foot becomes the skating foot. Practise this repeatedly from foot to foot.

There is a difference, however, when you are skating a crossed chassé backwards. When skating forwards the free foot is crossed behind the skating foot, whereas when skating backwards the free foot is crossed in front, i.e. the calf

35, 36. Crossed chassé from the front, with feet crossed and the skating foot lifted prior to replacement on the ice.

of the free leg is placed across the shin of the skating leg. So this time, for 'dry' practice, stand on your right foot with your left foot extended forwards; draw your left foot back across the front of your skating foot, place it on the ground, transfer your weight on to your left foot and then return to your original position. Repeat this in both directions until the movements are second-nature to you, then put on your skates and try it out on the rink.

PROGRESSIVES

Frequently also called a 'run', this term refers to a movement in which the free foot passes the skating foot and is then placed on the rink, with the original skating foot becoming the free foot trailing behind. Without skates on the movements are: starting on your left foot skating, bring your right foot forwards past the skating foot and, as you step on to your right foot, lift your left foot and let it assume a 'free' foot position behind your right foot.

BACKWARD CROSS-OVERS

As might be expected, backward cross-overs are the reverse of the forward movements, but there must be a constant lean into the circle. Let us take the cross-over going in the general direction of rink skating, i.e. in an anti-clockwise direction. Remember that the inside shoulder and arm must be pressed back, whilst the outside shoulder and arm should be a little higher and held in front of you. Photographs 37-39 explain what to do. Push on the right outside edge backwards and glide on the cross-over.

37-39. Backward cross-over. The free foot is crossed in front of the skating foot, which is lifted into the normal skating position, and the stroke taken from the crossed-in-front foot on to the outside back edge of the original skating foot. The sequence is: back outside, back inside crossed in front, and back outside. You must turn into the curve when skating solo, with open hips. The skater is going from right to left across the page.

SKATING TO MUSIC

So far we have progressed by learning the skating strokes, curves and simple chassés, but the real beauty of skating lies in skating your edges and turns, or whatever, to music. At first this will be merely skating forward and stroking in time to the music; later you will learn the dance steps and how to keep time to the appropriate rhythm. This may be accompanied by a strong desire to free skate, using your own steps and edges, to music of your own choice.

One hears about skaters 'interpreting' music; this is not strictly so, unless they are skating in a show. A skater expresses his reaction to the music. It is easy to refer to musical interpretation but it would be more accurate to talk about 'musical expression'. Choose music, whether it be pop or classical, that inspires you to skate and create your own programme.

If you are going to dance on skates, you will find a great difference from ballroom dancing. Whereas dance steps are taken on the rhythmic beat (except for certain poses in modern Latin American and ballroom dancing), as a skater you will find that you may have to hold an edge or change of edge for several beats! Again, whereas in ballroom dancing one learns steps and then puts them together in a sequence, in skate dancing the free dancing is limited to the higher proficiency tests, competitions and championships. Modern ice dancing is more like modern sequence and Old Tyme dancing in that the steps are approved in a certain sequence, and the patterns have to conform (in the majority of dances) to a certain design on the rink. There are, in effect, three types of set dance: (a) the set pattern in which certain steps always take place at specifically identified places on the rink; (b) the preferred pattern dance in which different patterns may be used, but in which the dancers must maintain the repetition; (c) a border dance, which is progressive around the rink.

First of all, it is necessary to learn to stroke and hold edges to the different rhythms and tempi. Suppose we commence with the waltz tempo. It is best to begin with waltz music at 3/4 at 45 bars per minute. This is the tempo for the European Waltz, though other waltzes have the music and tempi approved at 3/4 at 58 bars per minute (e.g. Starlight Waltz), 3/4 at 66 bars per minute (American Waltz), and 3/4 at 54 bars per minute (Westminster Waltz).

Assume your customary T-position for the start and wait for the music to begin. Do not start your first stroke until there is a *strong* beat on which to commence. Listen to the music carefully and count out the time as you skate from edge to edge 1-2-3 (LFO 1-2-3, RFO 1-2-3), etc.

When you feel that you are keeping in time to the music, you should also feel a good rise and fall of the skating knee so that you develop a soft knee action. All jerkiness must disappear: your skating must be smooth and in time to the music from edge to edge and from stroke to stroke. When skating to music, all steps must be made from heel to heel, and shoulders and hips must be held in a parallel position.

As the music helps you with the rise and fall and striking, you will also find that you will acquire stronger edges, i.e. the curvature will be greater. *Do not progress in a straight line when skating to music.*

Having skated forwards to waltz time, turn and skate your edges backwards to the same music, remembering of course to keep a watch to the rear so that you do not collide with another skater or even the barrier! It is impossible to keep time, if your stroking is wrong. The main difficulty in keeping time for many skaters seems to be that they are ahead of the music, i.e. they skate out of time by being too fast. Rarely, if ever, is a skater behind the music. The golden rule is: hold back until you feel that it is almost too late and then execute the movement – 100/1 you will then be in time – this is particularly so where turns have to be made, as there is a tendency to turn too early.

In free skating, as opposed to dancing, the skater does not have to keep in time to the music but uses it to harmonise the skating movements (jumps, spins, spirals, etc.,) into one rhythmic whole. So, *on the rink* practise running, stroking and curving to the music; *off the rink*, listen to music and even try to visualize skating to it – walk about at home and try to keep time to the music. After a while, no matter what the music is, whether film or television music, classical or pop, you will suddenly find yourself thinking, 'I'm going to skate to that' – you will then be well on the way to becoming an *interesting* skater, as opposed to the constant lapper round the rink.

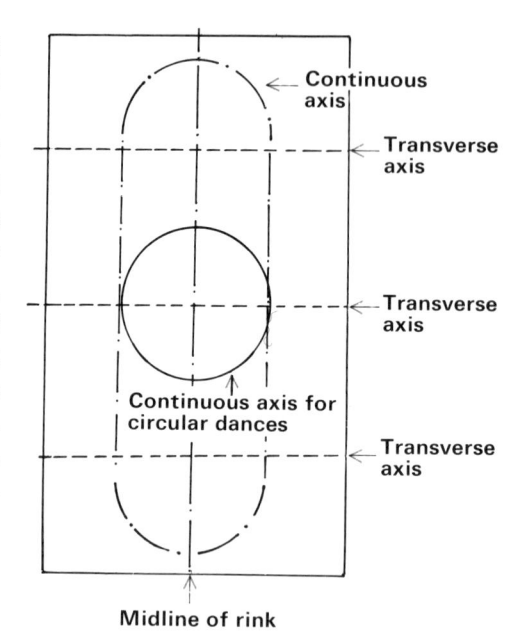

40. Placement of dance steps and edges on a rink must conform to patterns.

Just as the figure skater has to learn about the long and transverse axes for his figures, so, too, the dancer has to learn the terminology about placement of the dance steps. Reference will be made to the rink '*midline*' – this is, as it suggests, an imaginary line running the length of the rink and bisecting it into two equal parts (see diagram 40). The *continuous axis* is the imaginary line which runs around the rink in relation to which the pattern of the dance is made. Thus, in circular dances the continuous axis is a circle, and in other dances it usually consists of two straight lines down each side of the rink connected by semi-circles at each end. As in figures, the *transverse axis* is that which intersects the continuous axis at right-angles.

It is at this stage that you will find the disciplines diverging: dancing, on the one hand, requiring a partner, and figure skating, on the other, which may be performed solo, though a partner is necessary for pair figure skating. With the acquisition of easy, sure movements over the rink in time to music, we now turn our attention to the 'school' or 'compulsory' figures previously referred to.

5. The Basic Eights

There are four basic circle eights. These are: forward outside, forward inside, backward outside, and backward inside. They are performed on either foot.

FORWARD OUTSIDE EIGHT (Rfo-Lfo)

This figure, known as the Curve Eight, is performed on one foot on each half of the figure. That is, the first circle is skated on the right foot and the second circle on the left foot (see diagram 41). The abbreviation for skating this figure is: Curve Eight Rfo-Lfo.

When skating these Eights, no preliminary steps are allowed to gain impetus – they must be started from 'rest' and the *stroke must be clean and taken from the side of the blade, not from the toe*. No exaggerated posture or contortion of the body is permitted. When one circle has been completed and the skater is about to commence the second, the change from right to left skating foot (or vice versa) must be made without any pause.

Take up your position at the point where the two imaginary circles will meet to form the eight. Your right foot should be pointed in the starting direction of the circle and your left foot at right-angles, so that a good push-off can be made. Turn your body sideways so that you are in Position A, i.e. your right shoulder must be leading, with your left shoulder held well back. Your arms should be as shown in photograph 43. Your right hip will be forward and your left hip held back. In other words, you are sideways to the motion. Now thrust from your left skate with a slightly bent right knee, extending your left leg. As you start on the curve, your left leg should be kept slightly bent and

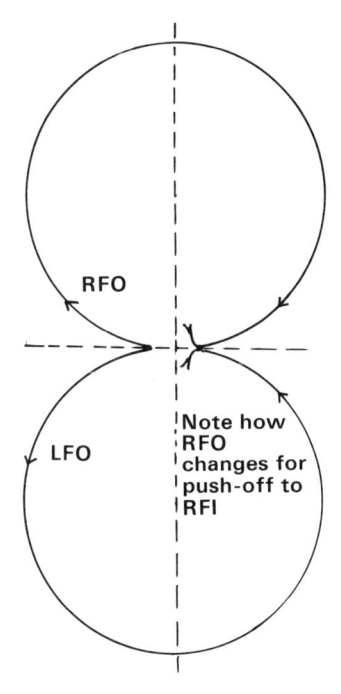

41. Rfo-Lfo circle eight.

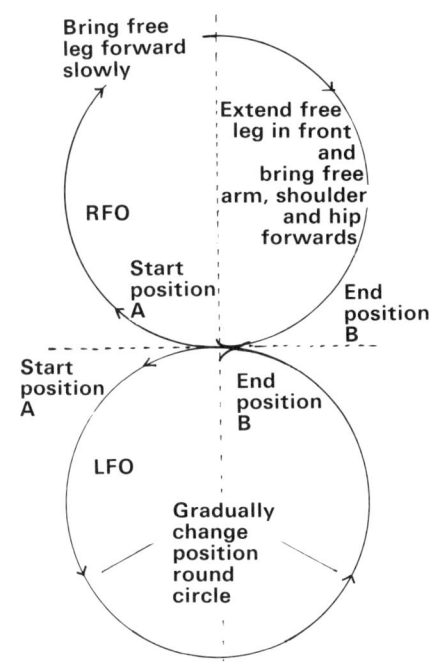

(Labels: RFO, LFO, Note how RFO changes for push-off to RFI)

42. Rfo-Lfo circle eight body positions.

(Labels: Bring free leg forward slowly; RFO; Start position A; Extend free leg in front and bring free arm, shoulder and hip forwards; End position B; Start position A; End position B; LFO; Gradually change position round circle)

over the line your right skate is making. Keep your head up and look over your right shoulder at your line of travel.

Once you have started on your edge, keep your right knee or tracing knee relaxed and slightly bent. Because your skating position has to be completely reversed by the time you complete the circle, so that you may strike out properly on the left foot, you must gradually start to shift your body and arms into the new position. Hold Position A until you have gone about one-third the way round the circle, then gradually bring your left leg (the free leg) forward. Do not move your hips. Continue to bring your left foot forward until it passes your right foot and is extended in front and over the imaginary skating tracing. About two-thirds of the way round the circle, bring your arms and shoulders round so that your right arm and shoulder commence to rotate back, and your left arm and shoulder come forward, and also gradually bring your free (left) hip forwards, ending in Position B (see diagram 42).

43. The starting position for the forward outside eight on the right foot.

You will now, at the completion of the first circle, be in the correct position to commence the second. This second circle is done in exactly the same way as the first one. Each figure, in tests and competitions, has to be skated three times, so when the second time round is commenced on the right foot this is termed 're-tracing' the figure.

There are certain rules which must be adhered to: the area where the change from one foot to the other is made must be kept to a minimum; circles must not overlap; curves have to be skated without wobbles or sub-curves; curves or circles must be uniform in size, and long and transverse axes must be maintained. As you become more proficient, you must strive to trace the figure laid down without sacrificing position.

You will find it helpful at this stage to trace the photograph showing the four basic positions A, B, C and D (p. 32 and 33) on to thin card. Then cut out the skating figures or leave them on a narrow piece of card. Bend a base under or add a small tab at the back; then draw out the circles on a sheet of paper and place the appropriate cut-out in its correct place on the circle. By doing this and also by taking up the positions in front of a mirror, when practising 'dry', you will soon become familiar with the correct skating positions.

Though we have referred to four basic skating positions, you will find in practice that the forward outside edge uses Positions A and B, the outside back uses B and A in that order, and the inside back uses B and A in that order, whilst the inside forward uses C and D in that sequence. The edges do, of course, use all the positions, notably C and D, for executing certain turns and advanced movements.

FORWARD INSIDE EIGHT (Rfi-Lfi)

This figure uses Positions C and D for commencement and completion of the circle (see diagram 45). In the Forward Outside Eight you started with your back to the circle so that you were leaning to the outside. In the Forward Inside Eight the lean is to the inside. The starting foot is the right foot, but the direction this time is anti-clockwise.

Take up your starting position with your right foot pointing in the direction of the curve to be skated. Position C is assumed with your right shoulder, arm, free leg and hip back. Your left arm will be leading. Look forwards and slightly over your left shoulder. Push off and hold this position until you have completed the first $\frac{1}{3}$ of the circle, at which point you gradually rotate your shoulders so that your right arm leads (see diagram 45). During this rotation, your hips remain stationary. Approaching the final $\frac{1}{3}$ of the circle and preparing for the change of foot, your left leg should slowly come forward close to your skating foot and turn out so that it lies across the print you are going to make. Your hips gradually assume a forward position and, as you approach the close of the first circle, your left foot should be ready to be placed on the ice on to the left forward inside edge. Thus you will already be in a reversed position, ready to strike off into the second circle on your left skate.

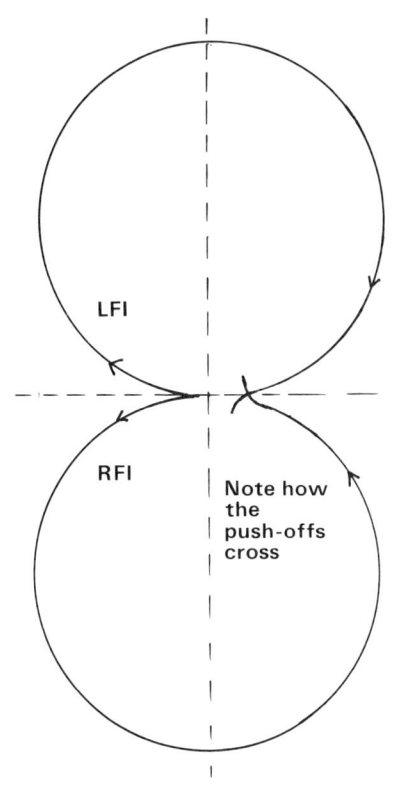

44. Rfi-Lfi circle eight.

BACK OUTSIDE EIGHT (Rbo-Lbo)

The main difficulty in skating this figure lies in the complicated push-off required (see diagram 50).

Take up your position to commence the figure with both feet on the rink, with your full weight on the left skate. Your right foot should be slightly further forward than your left foot, with the toe pointing downwards and just resting on the rink surface. Assume a position in which your left shoulder is drawn back and your right is forward, bend your left knee strongly and then push off

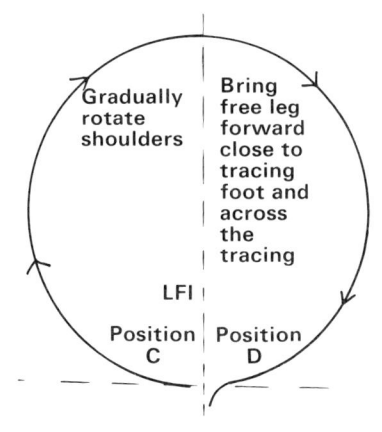

45. Rfi-Lfi circle eight body positions.

49

Direction of skating

46. Back outside eight commenced from rest.

47. Striking on to the edge.

48. Skating the first part of the circle.

49. Skating the second half of the circle and preparing for push-off on to second half of figure.

50. Rbo-Lbo circle eight.

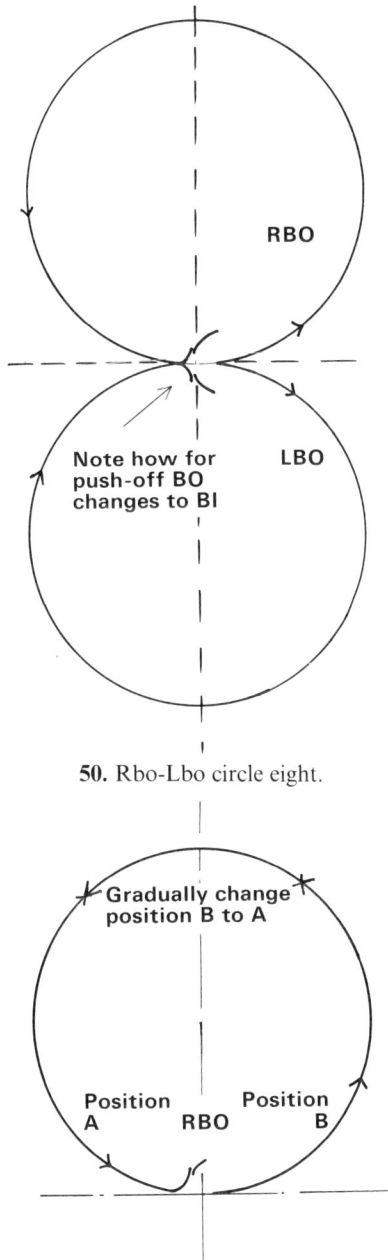

51. Rbo-Lbo circle eight body positions.

backwards on to your right skate (see diagram 51). As soon as the strike is made, lift your left foot. You should be looking over your left shoulder and your hips should be square. For a brief moment, your shoulders will be perpendicular to the tracing and your left leg should be held fairly close to your skating leg. Now reverse your shoulders and assume Position B, with your tracing shoulder and arm (right) back, whilst your free (left) shoulder, arm, hip and leg are forwards. You now look over your right shoulder. About half-way round the circle, you have to prepare to make the second circle. Gradually assume Position A with your free shoulder, arm, leg and hip drawn back and your right (tracing) shoulder and arm forwards.

When the circle is completed, your shoulders should be parallel to the transverse axis, ready for the push-off on your left foot. To prevent over-rotation, allow your shoulders to relax from the parallel position, and bring your left foot to the starting point and push-off from your right foot. The striking position should be identical with the original push-off from rest. Make certain that you close your circles, i.e. bring the first circle right up to the start of the second one and, above all, do not double-track, that is skate part of the change-over from one circle to the other with both skates on the rink.

BACK INSIDE EIGHT (Rbi-Lfi)

The push-off for this figure (see diagram 52) is much the same as for the Back Outside Eight, except that you lean inwards over the skate. It is important that you pick up your left skate immediately and that your right blade catches a very definite inside edge. Adopt Position B for two-thirds of the circle then gradually assume Position A. Remember, however, to change the position of your head (see diagram 53).

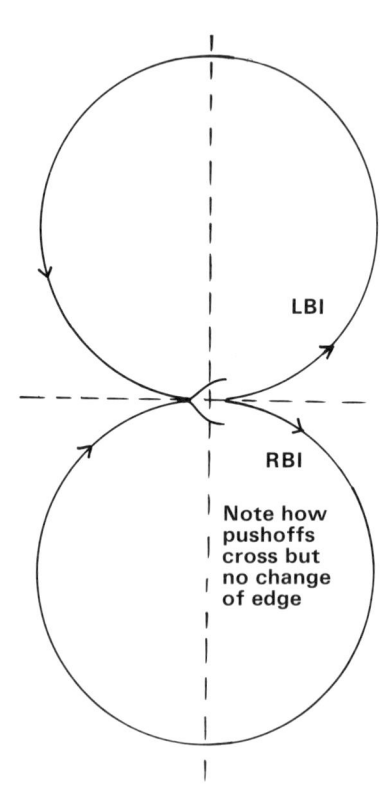

52. Rbi-Lbi circle eight.

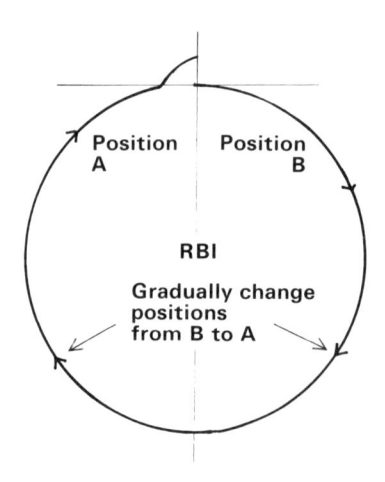

53. Rbi-Lbi circle eight body positions.

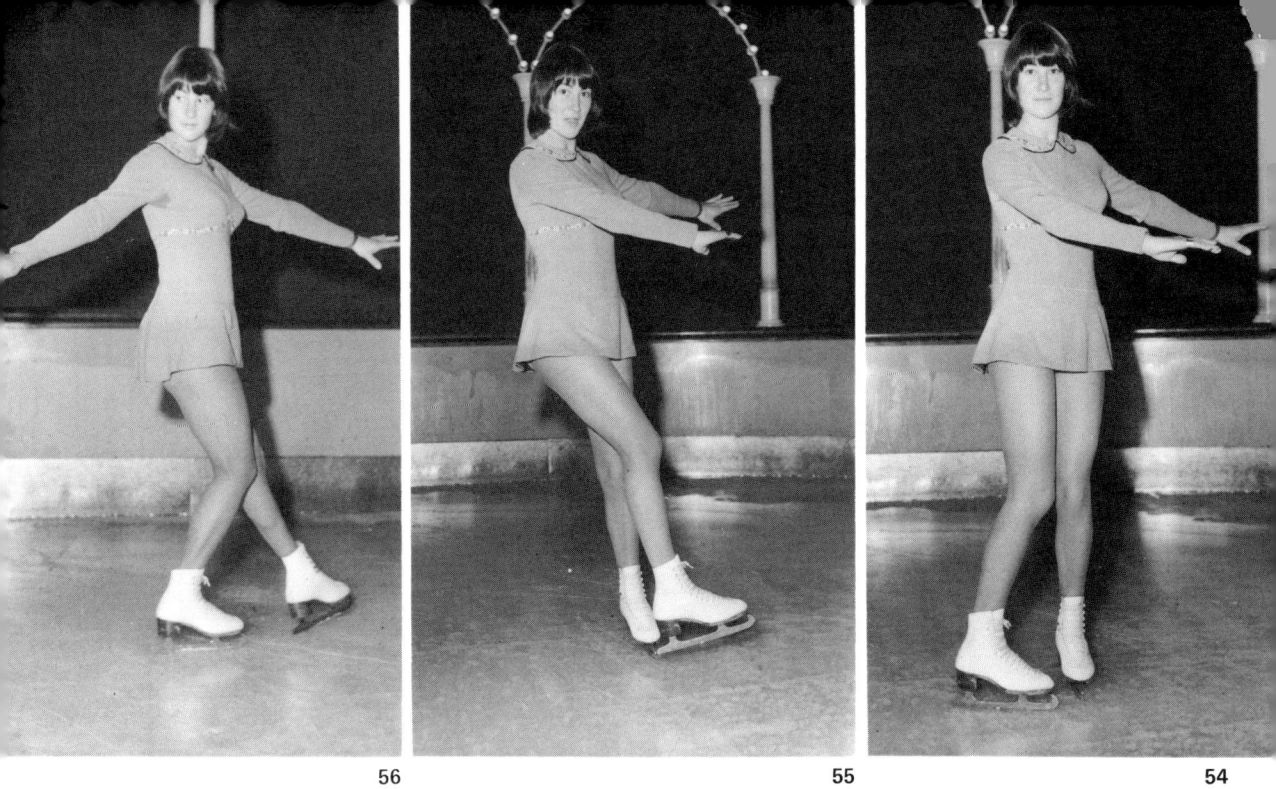

                56   55   54
            ←——direction of skating
54-56. The start of a back inside curve eight from rest.

CHANGES OF EDGE

These may be defined as movements performed on one foot in which the skater changes from one edge to the other.

Changes of edge are of two types (see diagram 57): the three-lobed serpentine figure and the two-circle Eight skated on one foot (the one-foot Eight) which is a rather advanced figure. The change of edge serpentine, which consists of a half-circle, a change on to the opposite edge for a full circle, then a change of foot followed by a half-circle, change, and full circle, is the next step in skating edges.

Changes of edge are used in free skating to link movements and also in dancing, where a change can be very slight indeed. Very advanced figures incorporate a change in their structure, e.g. loop-change-loop, change edge double loop, change bracket.

Basically, the change of edge consists of one half of a Curve Eight with the

53

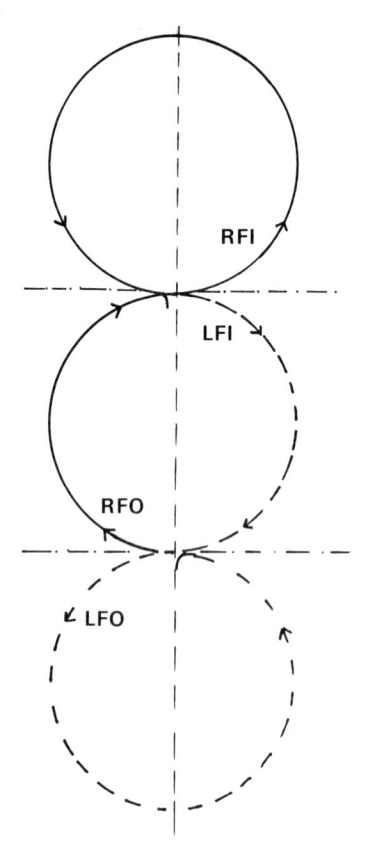

57. Change of edge: Rfoi-Lfio.

change of body and leg position and preparation for the thrust on to the other leg carried out on one foot only. A good rise and fall on the skating knee is essential, and the whole character of a good change of edge depends on the incorporation of the bending and straightening of the skating knee before, during, and after the change, with the correct body positions. If you are already able to skate the Curve Eights correctly, the changes of edge should present no difficulties.

FORWARD CHANGES OF EDGE (Rfoi-Lfio: Lfoi-Rfio)

Start the first semi-circle on the forward outside edge as for the Curve Eight, but, instead of waiting until you are well round the circle before you bring your free leg forward, slowly bring your free leg past your skating leg at one-quarter of the circle. Do not move your shoulders.

When the semi-circle has been skated on the outside edge, you change your lean from out of the completed half-circle into the circle about to be made. This is done by taking up the position of the start of an Inside Forward Eight, i.e. with your free shoulder and arm leading. The actual change will be little more than a skate's length and this should be straight along the tangent of the two circles (see diagram 62). There will, at first, be either or both of two tendencies: to go out of line either by curving in too much, or by skating at an

58–61. Change of edge from outside forward to inside forward: commencing from rest (58); the fo position (59) is changed by bringing the free leg forward (60) and completed (61) by taking the free leg back and assuming the forward inside position with free shoulder and arm leading.

angle across the tangent. A simple exercise to correct this error, using the free leg and foot, is easily learned. At one-quarter of the circle, swing your free foot so that first of all it points towards the centre of the circle after the change of edge. Your free leg should be fully extended just before the change itself. At the moment of change, swing your free leg back towards the centre of the completed half-circle. After the change, you complete the inner-edge circle, just as you would the ordinary Inside Forward Eight.

Having completed the first half of the figure (Rfoi), you now commence the next half of the figure (Lfio). Make a normal push-off on to the inside forward edge. A quarter of the way round the circle, bring your free leg forward and at the same time reverse your shoulders so that your body position is identical with that at the completion of the simple inside curve.

Make the change at the completion of the half-circle. Bring your free leg up in front and then back, and at the same time reverse your shoulders. You will now be on an outside edge. The body position is different from starting the normal outside edge and approximates to the final position of the ordinary Outside Edge Eight. You must hold this position throughout the whole of the circle, but bring your free leg forward during the last $\frac{1}{3}$ of the circle so that you will be ready to take-off on to the forward outside edge on the other foot and commence the figure over again.

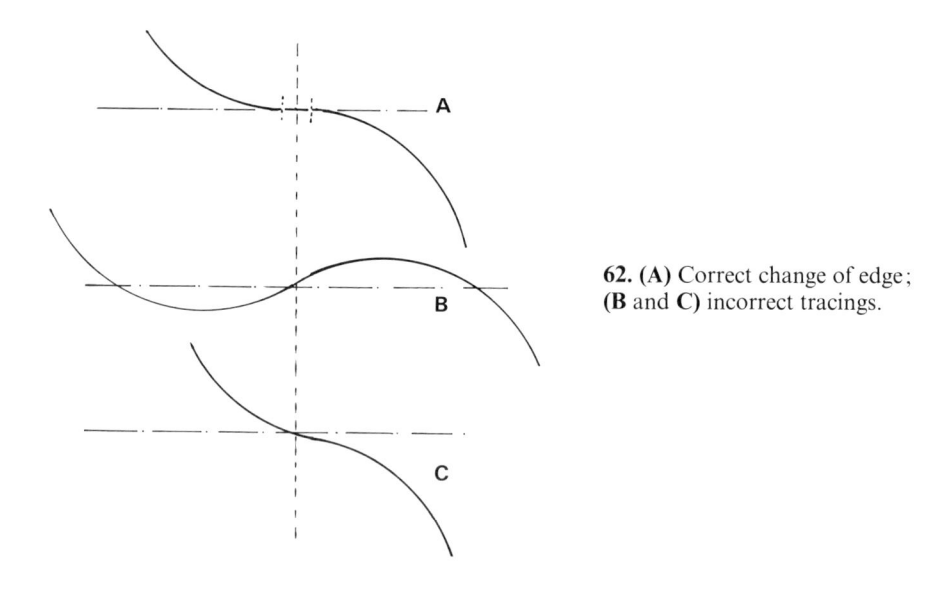

62. (A) Correct change of edge; **(B** and **C)** incorrect tracings.

BACKWARD CHANGES OF EDGE (Rboi-Lbio: Lboi-Rbio)

These are more difficult than the forward changes. You must use the same basic principles of change, and the use of the free leg is similar to that in forward changes. After the push-off on to the back outside edge, which is done in the normal way, keep your free leg close to your tracing leg and keep your tracing arm and shoulder forward. But, here is the main difference: do *not* look over your free shoulder – look to the inside of the circle you are making towards the spot where the change will be made.

On commencing the second half of the figure on the back inside edge, hold the circle as in the ordinary figure, with your free leg passing your skating leg at the $\frac{1}{4}$ mark of the first circle. Swing your free leg over the tracing you are about to make, then lift your skating shoulder slightly higher and hold it there until after the change is made. The moment you are on the outside edge, lower this shoulder, swing your free leg back, and stretch your free arm across your chest. You must hold this position (which checks the body and holds it on the edge properly) until you are $\frac{2}{3}$ round the circle, then gradually take up the position of an ordinary back outside edge and hold this till the close of the circle.

These changes of edges should first be practised 'in field' to acquire smoothness of movement and the necessary soft knee action, and to practise the different head positions involved.

Important

No matter what session you are skating in, whether private or public, you should make it a definite and rigid rule to practise your four simple edges *every time you skate* and to concentrate on neatness of footwork. Neatness of footwork and softness in the knee action cannot too strongly be emphasised. Remember, too, to keep your arms low. All too often one sees experienced skaters, skate dancers usually, who stretch their arms out in line with their shoulders. This is not necessary and does, in fact, look slightly ridiculous!

6. Turns

There are a limited number of turns in skating – they are divided into:

(a) One-footed movements in which the skater turns from forwards to backwards (or vice versa) whilst skating continuously on one foot.

(b) Two-footed movements in which a change from forwards to backwards (or vice versa) is accomplished with a change of foot.

ONE-FOOTED MOVEMENTS

These may involve a change of direction accompanied by an unchanged character of edge, e.g. from an outside forward edge to an outside back edge, or accompanied by a change of character of edge, e.g. from an outside forward edge to an inside back edge. There are also rotational changes to take into account. A natural rotation is one in which the body turns in the same direction as the curve being traced. A reverse rotation is one in which the body turns contrary to the direction of the tracing curve.

One-footed turns are: Three Turns, Brackets, Counters, and Rockers. You will only be concerned with the Three Turns performed on an outside forward edge to an inside back edge. The other turns are more advanced and require tuition from a professional coach. But, for the record, we shall identify the turns.

63. Three Turn.

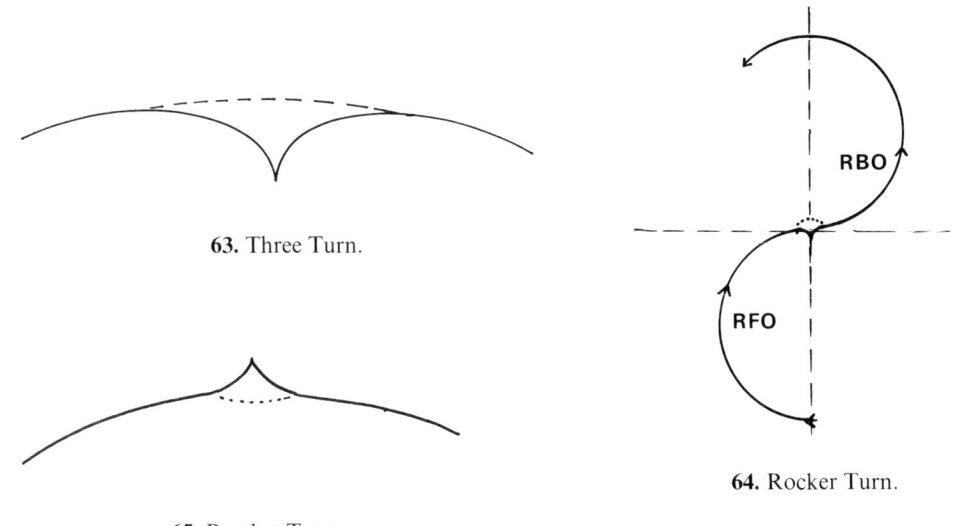

64. Rocker Turn.

65. Bracket Turn.

The Three Turn

Diagram 63 shows this turn on one foot, changing the direction of the skating from forwards to backwards, or backwards to forwards, and accompanied by a change of character of the edges. The rotation is natural and follows the curve of the circle. The edges change from inside to outside, or from outside to inside.

The Rocker

Diagram 64 shows a change of direction as in the Three Turn with a natural rotation for the first curve; the following unchanged character of edge in the second circle has a change of rotation.

The Bracket

This is performed on one foot (diagram 65), as in the Three Turn, but the turn is made against the natural rotation of the curve, i.e. the edges are of different character and the turn is reversed.

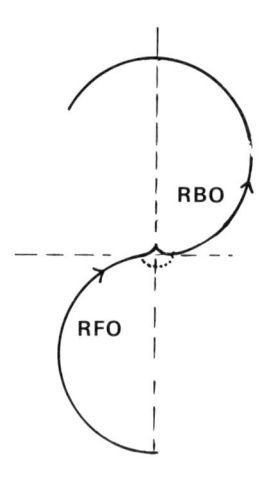

66. Counter Turn.

The Counter

This, as the name suggests, involves a counter or reverse direction of rotation (diagram 66). This is a change of direction from forwards to backwards, or from backwards to forwards, and is the reverse of the Rocker in that the two symmetrical curves forming the figure are skated with the turn in a reverse rotation, whilst the second has a natural sense of rotation. The edges are of the same character.

The abbreviations used to describe these Turns are as follows: T = Three; RK = Rocker; C = Counter; B = Bracket. Coupled with the abbreviations noted earlier, the following abbreviations would indicate:

RfoTbi = Right forward outside Three to back inside edge.
RfiBbi = Right forward inside Bracket to back inside edge.
LfoRKbo = Left forward outside Rocker to back outside edge.

One-footed turns are incorporated in the Compulsory Figures and are featured in the Schedules of Figures. They are skated in eight or paragraph form, and in the very advanced figures may also incorporate two different kinds of turn, e.g. Bracket-Rocker-Bracket.

TWO-FOOTED MOVEMENTS

These moves are simpler to define. They are, basically, the *Mohawk*, which involves a change from forwards to backwards or backwards to forwards with edges of the same character. *Mohawks* are divided into the following categories:

Closed Mohawk

This is a Mohawk skated with tracings crossing, but with the feet not crossed. The free foot is placed on the rink along the outer edge of the heel of the tracing foot. When the weight is taken on to the new skating foot; the free foot is in front of the toe of the tracing foot. The hip position is closed.

Open Mohawk

A Mohawk is performed by placing the free foot by the inside of the ankle of the tracing foot, the weight is transferred to the new skating foot and the foot that is now free is carried behind the heel of the skating foot. The open hip position which follows gives the Open Mohawk its name.

67. Closed Mohawk, about to transfer from inside forward edge on left foot to . . .

68. Inside back edge on right foot. Note the free foot in front of the tracing foot after the movement.

69, 70. Open Mohawk: the skater on a left forward inside edge (69) is about to step on to the right back inside edge (70).

Mohawk turns are also classified and *Crossed* and *Uncrossed*. A *Crossed Mohawk* is one where the feet are crossed in front or behind, but the tracings do not cross. An *Uncrossed Mohawk* is one where the tracings cross, but the feet do not.

Swing Mohawk

This is an uncrossed type in which the free leg is swung forward past the tracing foot and brought back close to it, before changing feet. It may be Open or Closed.

Choctaw

This two-footed movement is a Turn from forwards to backwards (or vice versa) from one foot to another on edges of different character, e.g. outside to inside. The Choctaws are *Crossed, Uncrossed, Closed, Open* and *Swing*, as in the case of the Mohawks.

SKATING THE TURNS

Forward Outside Three

During this Turn you will skate from an outside forward edge to an inside back edge, rotating in the direction of travel. This is a very important turn because, if done badly, it can be just about the ugliest movement on ice.

Let us learn the Three Turn on the left foot first, because you will be following the direction of the rink skating. (Photographs 71-73).

Take up your T-position. Commence the figure as if you were skating a forward outside edge. Now hold your skating hip underneath you so that you can feel your weight going through it down to the skating foot. Press your free leg and hip back. Stand perfectly erect. There must be no lean other than into the circle. Now rotate your shoulders against your hips until you are skating with your free shoulder leading strongly. At this point, lower your free leg and foot so that, with the skate off the rink, they assume a T-position behind your right foot. Try to touch your free foot against the heel of your skating foot and, as you still increase the rotation of your skating shoulder, allow your weight to transfer momentarily to the ball of your foot. Your skate will lift at the back slightly and turn through 180° to backwards. As soon as your skate takes up the inside back edge, reverse your shoulder pressure, press your free hip and shoulder back, and lean inwards on to the edge.

The action of the knee of the skating leg is vitally important. You push off on to a strongly bent skating knee, then straighten your leg as you come to the turn. As your feet come together in the T-position, both knees should be straight. After the turn, when the inside back edge is assumed, you bend your skating knee again.

The body action is really quite simple: begin the turn with your skating side leading and end it with your free side leading. Your skating shoulder should be kept slightly down and the actual turn should be done very quickly.

Inside Mohawk

This is probably the simplest of all Turns to learn. You commence with an inside forward edge on one foot and step on to the inside backward edge of the other foot.

73. After the turn.

72. Immediately prior to the turn: note the body position.

71. Forward outside three turn: skating the edge up to the turn.

Begin, as usual, in the T-position. Push off on to an inside forward edge, keeping your skating knee well bent. As you will be skating on your right foot for this lesson, press your left shoulder, arm, and free foot back over the tracing edge. Now draw your free foot towards the heel of your right foot, at the same time bending your free knee. Your toes should be turned out as much as possible so that your heels are drawn together. Touch the inside of your skating heel with your free heel. Now, reverse the pressure against your shoulders and allow your body to turn to the left. Quickly transfer your weight on to your left skate and at the same time slide your right skate away, in the direction of travel. Maintain a constant and steady lean to the inside of the circle.

The Mohawk which you have just skated is an Open Mohawk and is used in dance skating and extensively in free skating.

7. Dance Skating (Simple Dances)

As explained earlier, dance skating consists of a series of set steps rather like Old Tyme and sequence dancing in a ballroom.

It is necessary first of all to find a partner who will suit you for height, weight, and skating ability. Nothing looks more ridiculous than a tall man trying to ice skate with a tiny girl partner, or a small man being pulled along by a strong, well-built female! During the public sessions and at club sessions you will, of course, skate with a variety of partners, from experts to downright novices. However, to get the maximum enjoyment and benefit from dance skating partners should 'match' both physically and in skating ability.

Before attempting to dance with each other, you should spend considerable time running round the rink together in time to different rhythms. The correct holds should be learned and the couple should move round the rink together, using the various holds, occasionally changing from side to side. Because two people are skating together, the need to hold free legs over the tracing becomes apparent, as legs pushed out to the side soon trip a hapless partner and bring both parties to earth with a crash.

You and your partner should strive for the same knee action, your heads must move neatly and in unison, and the whole effect should be effortless. Footwork, too, must be neat, and free legs and feet should match in height from the rink.

Movements such as Three Turns, chassés, etc., should be practised together with the extended arm hold so that distance can be maintained and yet you will always be 'in touch'. The man must be prepared to show off his lady to advantage and become a background figure; this is also essential in pair skating.

THE DANCE HOLDS

Hand in Hand

In this position the couple face the same direction and skate side by side (see photograph 75). It is customary for the lady to be on the man's right.

74. Extended arm hold, usually employed for the opening steps of a dance; also useful for simple practice in maintaining distance in turns and movements for pair skating.

75. Hand-in-hand hold.

76. Waltz position.

Waltz Hold

This is also termed the 'closed' position. Partners face each other, one skating forwards, the other backwards. The man's right hand is placed firmly against the lady's back at the shoulderblade with the elbow raised and bent. She places her left hand on his right shoulder. The man's left arm and the lady's right arm are extended at shoulder height (see photograph 76).

Foxtrot Hold

This hold is sometimes called the 'open' position. Here the Waltz hold is used but the partners open into a V-position and skate in the same direction. This is rather like the Promenade position in ballroom dancing.

Tango Hold

In this hold the partners face in opposite directions. The hold is similar to the Waltz hold, but the partners do not skate directly opposite each other. They skate hip to hip, with the man on the left or the right of the lady. This is sometimes termed the 'outside' position.

79. Kilian hold.

80. Reversed Kilian hold.

Kilian Hold

The partners skate in the same direction, facing the same way. The man is on the lady's left, with her left shoulder against his right shoulder (see photograph 79).

Reversed Kilian Hold

This is identical to the Kilian Hold described above except that the man is on the lady's right. The Fiesta Tango is danced in this hold (photograph 80).

Variations of Kilian Hold

Other Kilian positions, used in advanced dances such as the Jamaican Rhumba, are the open position and the crossed position, which are of little interest or value to the beginner.

It should be pointed out that dances should be skated with as much expression as possible, edges should be strong, and you should show true rhythmic feeling, but, at the same time, the prescribed relationship of the edges to the patterns laid down must be maintained. When you dance on ice skates, show that you are enjoying yourself and be as relaxed as if you were dancing at a party or in a ballroom.

81, 82. Contrast the couple in these photographs in the Waltz hold. On the left their carriage is erect, their legs are matched, and they are close together, but on the right . . .

THE GLIDE WALTZ

This is a very pleasant dance to learn. Both partners skate forwards throughout and do the same steps. They skate side by side in the Kilian hold, with the lady on the man's right. The pattern is serpentine and open chassés are used on alternate feet.

The opening steps are a 3-beat edge to the left on an outside edge, followed by a 3-beat edge to the outside right. The start is followed by a chassé to the left on the outside edge (Lfo 2 beats: Rfi 1 beat), followed by a 3-beat edge on the left forward outside. There follows a chassé begun on the right forward outside (Rfo 2 beats: Lfi 1 beat) and an outside forward edge on the right foot for 3 beats.

When you and your partner, who skate with shoulders across the tracing throughout the dance, skate round the end of the rink, you skate an outer lobe chassé (Lfo: Rfi), followed by a right inside forward edge (Rfi) which is held for 3 beats.

Your free foot must never come ahead of your skating foot. Your carriage must be upright, your heads erect, and the toe of your free foot must be turned downwards and outwards. With a good knee bend and careful attention to the timing, the character of the waltz must be shown with a good expressive rise and fall of the skating knee.

83. Glide Waltz steps.

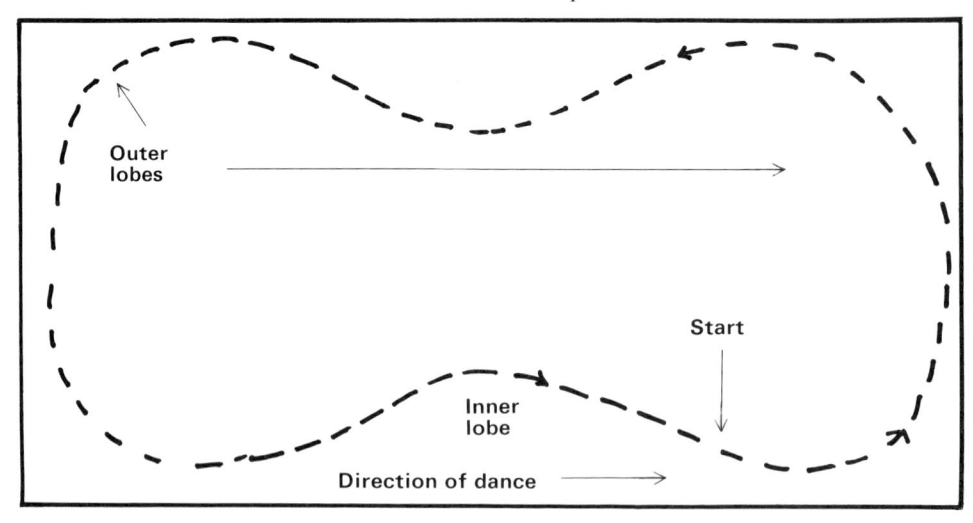

84. Rink pattern for Glide Waltz.

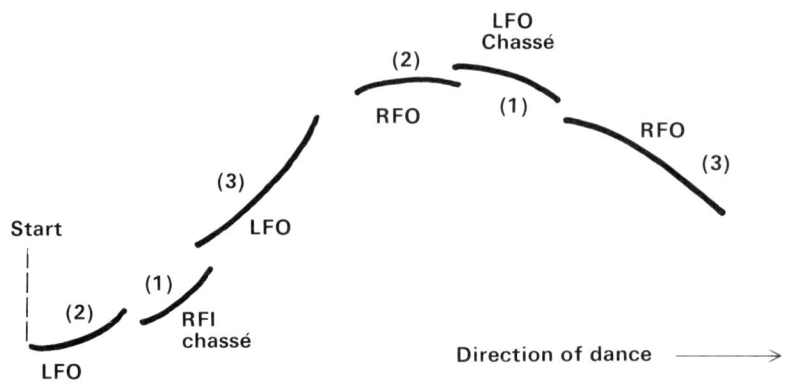

THE FOXTROT MOVEMENT

This is also called the Preliminary Foxtrot and forms a compulsory dance for candidates in the Preliminary Dance Test organized by the National Skating Association of Great Britain.

This dance is very simple, though it is a real test of skating proper edges with good style and carriage. During the dancing you must extend your free leg properly and see that your tracing leg bends and straightens well. The Foxtrot Movement is very pleasant to skate as a dance in its own right. It has the great advantage that both partners skate the same steps, which are forward only. Preliminary opening steps are allowed, not exceeding four, after which the dance starts. The tempo is 26 bars per minute in Foxtrot 4/4.

You and your partner assume the Kilian hold, with the lady on the man's right. After the preliminary steps have been completed, strike on to a left forward outside edge, followed by a right inside forward run and a left outside forward edge. On this step, both of you swing your free leg slowly forward, past your tracing feet. The edge is steepened and your skating legs should be bent. The next step is taken on to the right forward outside edge, followed by a left inside run, then a strong right forward outside edge and a forward swing of the left leg. The runs and swings are repeated alternately on each foot. The timing is 1:1:4 (left forward outside edge 1 : right forward inside edge 1 : left forward outside 4 – and so on alternately).

The couple should look towards the centre of the rink when skating on the left outside edge, and towards the barrier when skating the right forward inside edge.

It is excellent exercise to practise the Foxtrot Movement backwards in which you perform backwards progressives or runs, followed by an outside back edge during which the free foot is swung back slowly. You can also alternate skating backwards and forwards in Waltz Position.

8. More Advanced Dances

When you have successfully performed the simple steps of the elementary dances, it will be very useful if you and your partner learn each other's steps because, when you each begin to skate different steps, dancing becomes a little more complicated.

In order to link the various elements of skate dancing together you will find it helpful to learn the following dance, which makes use of open chassés, cross-overs and swinging of the free leg. When you have learned how to do it forwards, you can skate the dance backwards, changing the steps accordingly. I call it the St Ivo Tango Waltz, because I introduced it at the St Ivo Recreation Centre in Cambridgeshire. Though it is usually skated to Tango music, it may equally well be skated to Foxtrot, Blues, Waltz, and even Fourteen Step.

The dance is skated in the Kilian Hold with the lady on the man's right. You can either skate two or four opening steps, after which you both skate a forward outside edge on the left foot, followed by an outside edge on the right foot. Two quick strokes are made on the left outside and right outside (to suit the music chosen), and both of you then stroke on to an outside left forward towards the centre of the rink. You both skate an open chassé to the left, followed by an open chassé to the barrier. You both then skate an outside forward edge on the left foot, followed by a slow cross-over to inside right, then outside left followed by a slow forward swing of the right foot. The next step is outside forward to the right, towards the barrier, followed by a left inside edge crossed in front, a right outside edge and a slow forward swing of the left foot. After this, the sequence is repeated from the beginning.

THE EUROPEAN WALTZ

This is an International Dance which, although the steps are simple enough, is extremely difficult to learn correctly. You either skate it very badly or very well – it is that type of dance!

Basically the European Waltz consists of a Three Turn on the outside edge forwards, and of outside edges. The dance is skated in the Waltz position and the man must skate directly facing his partner throughout the dance on all strokes. The free foot must be kept close to the skating foot and, as the dance is skated in a series of lobes, those skated along the rink should be semi-circles. The number of lobes skated depends upon the length of the rink.

Man's steps

He starts with a left forward outside edge followed by a Cross Roll on the right forward outside edge and a Three Turn to back inside. After the Three Turn, the free foot is then placed on the ice close to, but *not* behind, the skating foot takes up a back outside edge.

Sequence: Lfo 3 beats
Cross Roll Rfo
Three Turn   2 beats
Rbi 1 beat
Lbo 3 beats

85. Pattern and steps for gentleman in European Waltz.

86. Steps for lady in European Waltz; quarter rink pattern.

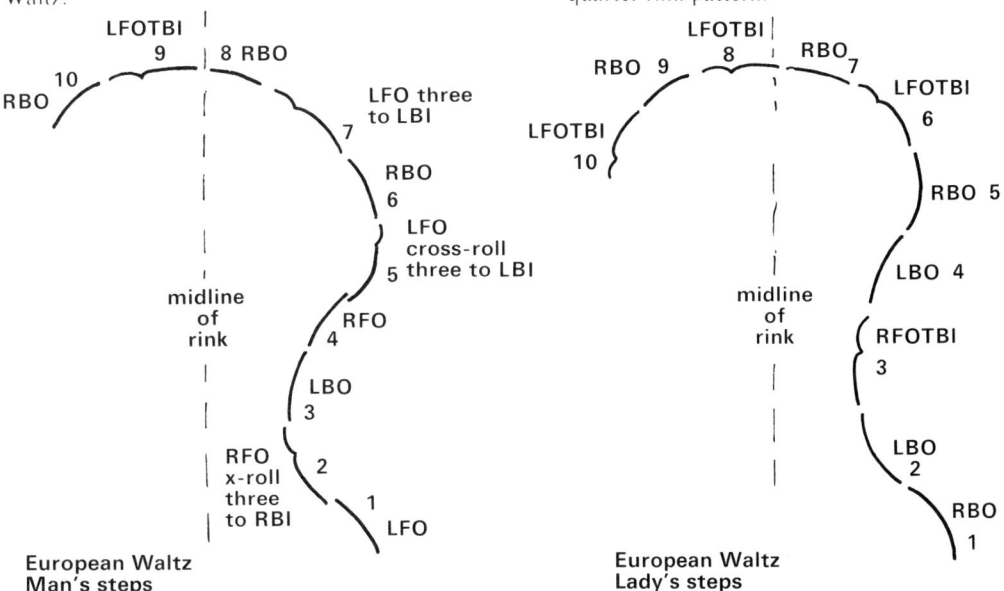

European Waltz
Man's steps

European Waltz
Lady's steps

The man then alters his steps so that he skates a right forward outside, followed by a left forward outside Cross Roll, a Three Turn to the left back inside edge, and a right back outside edge.

When skating round the end of the rink, the sequence is altered to a series of Lfo Three Turns to Lbi and Rbo, after which the man skates the opening Lfo followed by a Rfo Cross Roll and a Three Turn to Rbi.

Lady's steps

She starts with a Three Turn to take up the waltz position and, when the man skates his first Lfo and Cross Roll Rfo, she skates Rbo for 3 beats, followed by Lbo for 3 beats. She then steps forward to Rfo (2 beats) with a Three Turn to Rbi (1 beat) and backwards on to Lbo (3 beats). This Lbo 3-beat edge coincides with the man's step number 4, which is a 3-beat Rfo. Thereafter she skates on the opposite edges and turns until the end of the rink is reached. Whilst the man does his succession of Lfo Three Turns, she also skates the same. Each Lfo, Three Turn and Lbi should coincide with the Rbo of the man.

There is often discussion as to how many Three Turns should be skated round the edge of the rink; this depends upon the width of the rink, of course, and may vary from four to six, though on extremely narrow rinks only three may be possible. A feature of this dance is that it reverses its direction at the commencement of each new lobe and the partners rotate continuously round each other. Some slight checking is necessary after the Three Turns to prevent over-rotation and the lobes along the rink should be started either directly towards the barrier or directly away from it. Turns should be made *between* the partner's feet.

Faults to avoid

It is a horrible sight to see a couple trying to waltz by pulling each other round with the free leg bent at the knee and the free foot swinging at right angles! Concentrate on keeping your free foot close to your skating foot, even by placing it against the skating foot in a T-position just prior to the actual Three Turn – this will help a great deal in giving control and stopping you rotating too far. It is essential, too, that each partner stands perfectly upright. Any leaning forwards or backwards is to be avoided and every effort must be made to step from heel to heel when changing feet.

When the European Waltz is skated in a reverse direction round the rink, it is called the Reverse Waltz. The steps, sequences and timing are the same and should present no undue difficulty to the skater who has practised the edges and turns thoroughly, though oddly enough the Reverse Waltz daunts many dancers.

THE FOURTEEN STEP

This is a splendid dance! It makes good use of skating movements and techniques, and is a lively dance skated to march music at 3/4 or 6/8 at 56 bars per minute. The Fourteen Step is probably the oldest skating dance, having been invented by Franz Schöller in Vienna in 1889 and called the Schöller March. It has retained its popularity and is today skated in two versions; the British Fourteen Step, and the International Fourteen Step. However, the original dance only contained ten steps and was called the Ten Step; to-day, skaters still continue to refer to it as the Ten Step when describing either Fourteen Step version.

The version I refer to in these pages is the British Fourteen Step. I prefer to use the original British version when introducing this dance to pupils, because it is such an excellent basis for free skating. I insist that the man's and lady's steps should be learned by both partners to give practice in skating forward and backwards chassés, and the different Mohawks involved. The Fourteen Step dance entails soft knee action. It is danced in a circle, but does not have to conform to a set pattern. It is skated to a total of 18 beats and is 9 bars to a sequence (see illustrations 87 and 88).

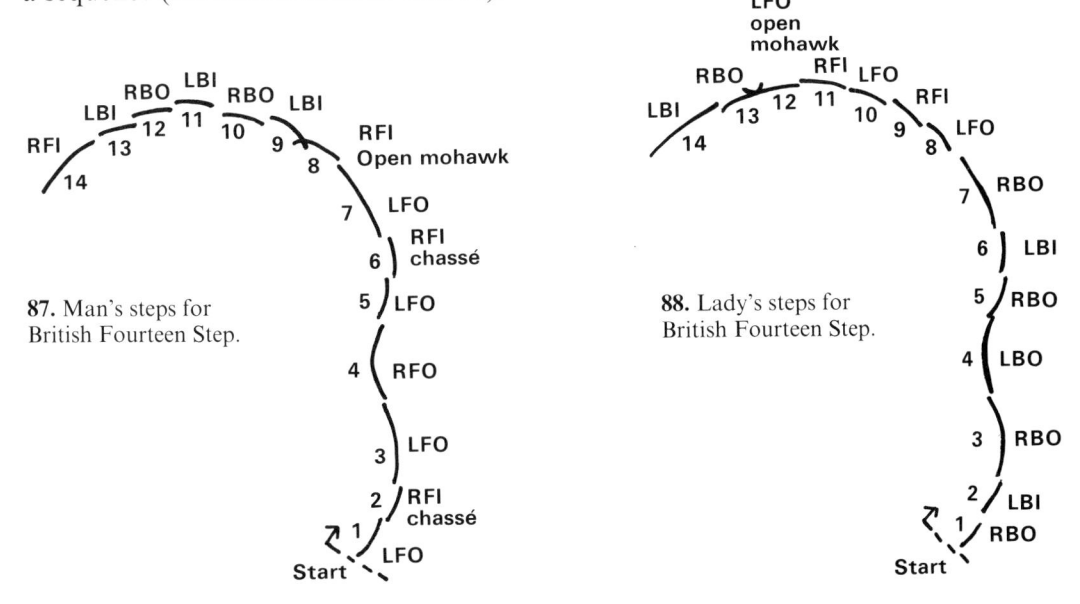

87. Man's steps for British Fourteen Step.

88. Lady's steps for British Fourteen Step.

Partners dance in the Waltz hold. The man commences by skating an open chassé (Lfo 1 beat: Rfi chassé 1 beat: Lfo 2 beats); at the same time the lady skates an outside back edge, followed by a crossed-in-front left back inside edge. As the man steps on to the forward outside 2-beat edge, she takes a right back outside edge for 2 beats (Rbo 1 beat: Lbi crossed-in-front 1 beat: Rbo 2 beats).

The fourth step is an Rfo for the man and an Lbo for the lady held for 2 beats. After which, the man repeats his open chassé (Lfo: Rfi chassé: Lfo) and the lady skates Rbo, followed by a crossed-in-front Lbi and an Rbo. After this seventh step which is held for 2 beats, the man skates an Rfi Open Mohawk to Lbi, whilst the lady turns forwards on an Lfo, followed by an Rfi crossed behind. The man then skates an Rbo, an Lbi run and an Rbo for 1 beat each, whilst the lady skates an Lfo run, followed by an Rfi run and an Lfo Open Mohawk to Rbo. Each of these steps is a 1-beat edge or turn. The man then does a backwards cross-over to an Lbi (1 beat) and steps forwards on to a 2-beat Rfi. Whilst the man crosses in front on to his left inside back edge, the lady skates an Rbo followed by an Lbi for 2 beats. This completes the sequence and the dance then recommences.

One common fault is the skating of the man's fourth step as an inside edge; this is quite wrong – it must be skated on an outside edge out of the circle.

The steps are as follows (beats are shown in brackets):

Man: Lfo (1) – Rfi chassé (1) – Lfo (2) – Rfo (2) – Lfo (1) – Rfi chassé (1) – Lfo (2) – Rfi Open Mohawk (1) to Lbi (1) – Rbo (1) – Lbi run (1) – Rbo (1) – Lbi crossed in front (1) – and Rfi (2).

Lady: Rbo (1) – Lbi crossed in front (1) – Rbo (2) – Lbo (2) – Rbo (1) – Lbi crossed in front (1) – Rbo (2) – Lfo (1) – Rfi crossed behind (1) – Lfo run (1) – Rfi run (1) – Lfo Open Mohawk (1) to Rbo (1) – and Lbi (2).

THE FIESTA TANGO

This is not commonly skated in Britain, which is a pity, because it is a very attractive dance. Both partners skate the same steps in the same forward direction. The author was introduced to it by an American ice skater. It makes use of the steps learned in the previous dances, including the British Fourteen Step.

The partners skate in the Reverse Kilian hold with the lady on the man's left. During the dance (see illustration 89) there is a change of position. The steps are:

Lfo – Rfo – Lfo chassé *or* progressive – Rfi – Lfo – Rfo crossed in front – Lfi crossed behind – Rfoi (change of edge) – Lfo – Rfi Open Mohawk to Lbi – Rbo – Lbi – Rbo – Lbi crossed in front – Rfi.

At the change of edge, both free legs must swing together with a good bend, rise, and bend of the knee. Immediately after the 6-beat swing change of edge, the lady moves slightly ahead of her partner on an Lfo in preparation for the Open Mohawk.

When the Mohawk is executed, the hold is changed from Reverse Kilian to Kilian, with the lady skating on the man's right. After the left inside back cross, in preparation for stepping forward to Rfi and repeating the dance, the position is shifted back to the Reverse Kilian hold with the lady on the man's left.

If you and your partner are ambitious, it is comparatively easy to learn the steps backwards as well, so that the dance becomes even more impressive. This dance is also a good basis for working into a free skating programme, particularly if the swing change edge is executed with spirit.

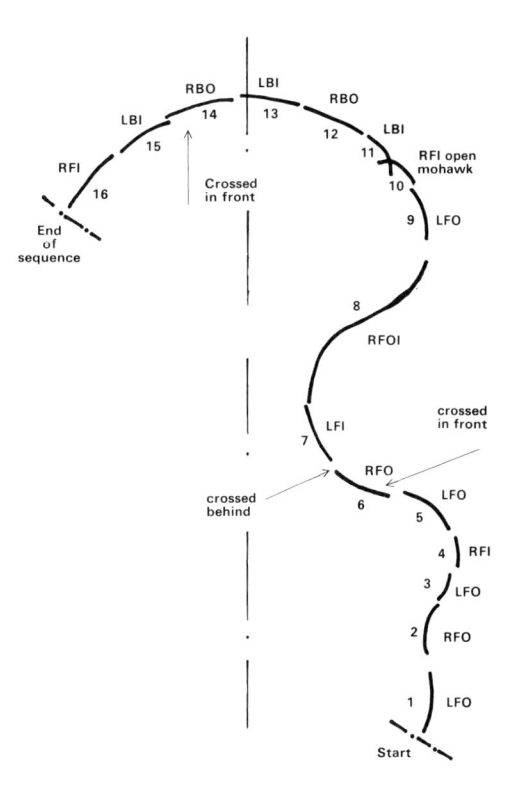

89. Steps and rink pattern for the Fiesta Tango.

9. Free Skating

Free skating includes both solo skating and pair skating. If you have ambitions to turn professional and skate for a living, the choice may lie between (a) teaching and (b) show skating. There is a desperate shortage of male skaters at the moment for both fields, but the qualifications are different. Many champions and successful competition skaters turn to show skating first, because they feel it is a continuation of their free skating. Others turn professional in order to teach. In either event, a good ability to perform free skating and dancing is necessary. However, for the coach it is also important to have a good knowledge of school figures and compulsory dances, and many vacancies specify the necessary qualifications as Silver or Second Class standards at least. Show skaters fall into the categories of individual acts, stars or supporting acts, and line or chorus skaters. Individual acts may include free skating, pair skating, dancing, or comedy and 'knock-about' numbers. For the line or chorus skater, it is necessary to be able to skate figures reasonably well and be able to execute simple jumps, lifts, and so forth.

Not all skaters, however, wish to take proficiency tests, win competitions, or turn professional. They skate for the sheer enjoyment of it – and free skating, performed solo, is an exhilarating experience. Movements in free skating include dance steps, linking steps from movement to movement, jumps, spins, spirals, Spread Eagles, arabesques and so on, but all free skating is based, intrinsically, on proper edges and body positions.

SPIRALS AND ARABESQUES

Most skaters, when confronted with the word 'spiral' immediately try to skate over one foot with the body bent forwards from the waist and the free leg held very high behind, but this is only one form of spiral – the arabesque. A spiral is an edge, skated on one foot, with the body erect, at a good speed and held for the minimum of one circle. The term spiral is used because, if an edge is held continuously, the radius of the curve decreases gradually and you skate a curve that gets smaller as the speed drops.

As a rule, male skaters skate their arabesques and spirals in a more upright position than female skaters. The latter may even be able to skate bent so far forwards that their head is well below the skating knee, with the free leg held high, and in continuous line with the spine. When skating an arabesque, the back should be arched so that the free leg and the head are higher than the body. There is no set position for the arms during a spiral or arabesque, but the golden rule is never to let your back slump. Your free foot must always be turned out and your toe pointed gracefully. The secret is in stretching to the fullest extent.

At the beginning you will tend to skate too far forward on your skate when performing a forward spiral; your weight must be well back, otherwise there is a danger of catching your toe-pick and of falling unexpectedly and heavily.

90. Arabesque skated on a spiral.

91. A simple two-footed jump.

96. Completion with extended free leg and rotation checked by free shoulder.

95. Landing on a back edge.

JUMPS AND SPINS

The first basic in jumping is the ability to leave the surface of the ice. The actual turning and rotation are of secondary importance, so begin by jumping on both feet. (See photograph 91, p. 79).

Skate forwards, bring both feet close together parallel to each other; now spring into the air from strongly bent knees. At the same time, lift your arms in front of you. You will jump a few inches into the air and, the moment you land, bend your knees and continue skating on both feet. Repeat this a few times until you are landing correctly over the skates, without your weight being tilted to either side.

Now, once again using the same take off, as you leave the rink surface, turn in the air to one side or another. You will describe a semi-circle and find yourself landing backwards. As you hit the ice, bend both knees and keep your feet parallel. Then extend your arms to the side. Try this until you are taking off and landing without wobbles or bending.

To jump from backwards to forwards; skate backwards, draw both feet close together and parallel again. Now, with body upright and head up,

94. In the air.

93. The free leg swings forward and the skating leg straightens at take-off.

← direction of skating

92. The Three Jump: preparation.

swing your arms to the front and spring upwards. *After you have sprung*, turn forwards. You will find that you turn easily in the air and will land on both skates, with knees well bent, in a forwards position. See that you land with your body in a perfectly upright position. You are now ready to tackle the simple jumps.

THE THREE JUMP

This is also called the Waltz Jump (see diagram 97). A true Three Jump is executed on one foot only, taking off from the outside edge and landing on the inside edge of the same skate. The Waltz Jump, however, is skated from a forward outside edge on one foot, turning in the air and landing backwards on an outside edge on the other skate.

Skate forward two or three short edges, then draw your feet together to get the feel of the take-off you have been making, i.e. get your knees bent and your body erect. Do this a couple of times, then skate boldly on to an outside edge on your left foot, swing your free foot forward past the skating leg in a straight

81

position as the jumping take-off point is reached and, at the same time, bring your right arm forward. The swinging forward of the leg and arm will assist in the 'lift'.

Now do not try to turn round to backwards! The lift-off is made as the free foot swings past the skating foot and the jump is made out of the circle, *not round it*.

As you land on to the right outside edge, bend your right knee strongly, and still keep an upright position of the body. Stop your shoulder from rotating by holding your left arm forward and your right arm back. This will prevent the edge on which you have landed from curling into a circle. Extend your left leg behind your right leg with the toe turned out.

Remember at all times to keep your body upright, the take-off and landing knees bent, and your head upright. *Do not try to turn until you have actually taken off in the jump.*

Once you can do this Three Jump, you have the basis of many other jumps. It is sound practice to skate a series of Three or Waltz Jumps in succession.

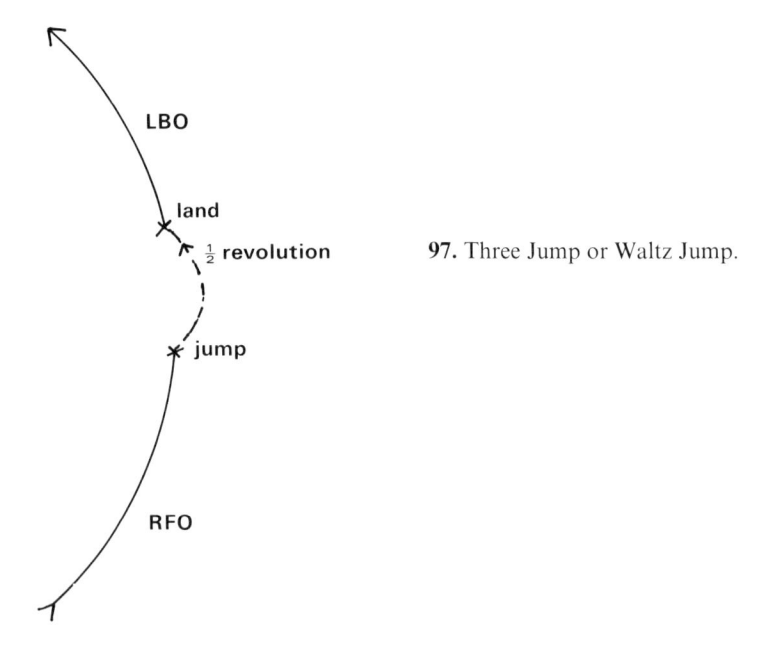

97. Three Jump or Waltz Jump.

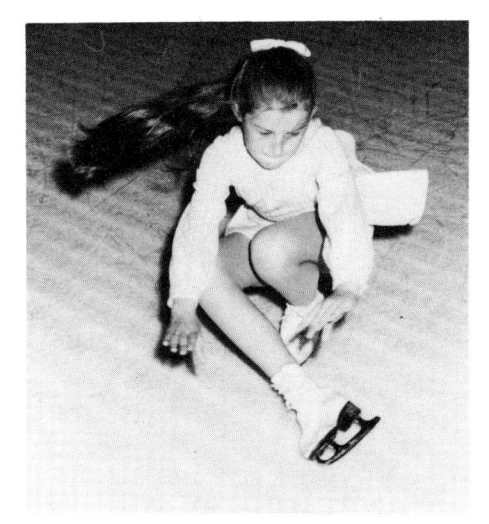

98, 99. The sit spin. Contrast the photograph on the left with that on the right: (left) the young skater has her free foot crossed over the spinning foot and her knee bent; (right) the skater is well down on the spin with free leg and arms gracefully extended.

SPINS AND PIROUETTES

Learning to spin is fun! The first problem is to learn to overcome the dizziness which follows the spin. However, in a remarkably short time you will get used to rotating and will be able to come out of even a long and fast spin without any giddiness or loss of direction. There are many different spins executed with the body in an upright position. They may be executed with the free leg leading or behind with partial use of the toe picks or on the flat of the blade.

Let us start with a simple spin on one foot on the flat of the blade. First of all, get on to a forward outside edge (most skaters use the right foot) and turn a Three to inside back. Allow your left shoulder to come forwards and press your right shoulder back. Step forwards on to your left foot on an outside edge, bend your skating knee strongly, straighten it, turn a Three to back inside and allow your right shoulder to come forwards while pushing your left shoulder back. As you commence the rotation which follows, straighten your skating leg and push down hard on to the ball of your foot. Keep your arms equally to the side and front. As the spin begins, bring your free leg to the front and gradually draw your arms in. As the free leg is brought forward and the arms drawn in, the rotation will increase in speed. To come out of the spin, open your arms.

100. In this very graceful spin the skater is holding her free foot in an arabesque position.

At first you will not actually spin, but will make a series of small circles which will gradually become even smaller and the spin will develop. The main difficulty of the spin is to 'centre' it, i.e. you must not travel off the original spot on which the spin started. The strong body rotation referred to will help you stay on the spot.

Once you have learned how to execute a spin on the flat of the blade, you can try the Scratch Spin, in which you rise on to the front part of the blade and use the toe picks. To complete a Scratch Spin you bring your free leg forward over the front of your skating leg and lower your foot, so that your free ankle lies above the instep of your spinning foot. This gives great speed in the spin.

DANCE STEPS

These are linking steps used to keep the skater moving about the surface in a free skating programme and to connect the various movements, spins, jumps, etc. being executed.

Movements such as continuous changes of edge, Mohawks, spirals and arabesques, and Spread Eagles are used. Provided they are intelligently employed to enable the skater to cover the whole of the skating area and balance the programme, the emphasis must be on originality and flexibility. It is very easy to copy the better skaters and acquire 'set' free skating steps. How much better to experiment and work out your own!

To begin with, the steps in the Fourteen Step used by the man have been referred to (p. 75) and it needs little effort to build on them. For example, after the inside forward Mohawk, you can then turn round completely and step forward on to the left outside edge and execute a Three Turn, followed by an outside back on the right foot, a cross-over left back inside and step forwards to right forward inside, cross behind left forward inside and do an inside Mohawk to back right inside.

To free skate effectively, you must be proficient in skating on both feet and able (apart from spins and jumps) to execute movements forwards and backwards, to right and left.

Pair skaters in particular need to practise running together and to execute steps and movements both in holds and in 'shadow', i.e. not touching. It is helpful to practise skating school figures together, jumping together to get the timing of take-off and landing right, and spinning apart. Good pair skating requires the constant supervision of a very experienced coach and this should be sought at the outset.

There are a number of movements (other than the ones already mentioned) which can help to express the music and to carry the skater in full coverage of the rink surface. Typical of such movements are the Teapot, the Drag, and the Spread Eagle.

THE TEAPOT

The Teapot is very popular with younger skaters and affords excellent training

101. A high-speed backward tea-pot is spectacular, and is often used in exhibitions and in free skating.

102. Forward shot of the Drag. It is sometimes done on completion of a jump or a sequence.

for the Sit Spin later. To skate a Teapot (photograph 101), get up a good speed skating forwards, then bend your skating knee and lower yourself so that you are in a squatting position. At the same time, bend your body forwards from the hips and extend your free foot straight forwards past your skating foot. This movement has the advantage that, if you should fall off it, you simply sit down on the rink. When you have mastered the forward Teapot, it it is exciting, and equally easy, to try a backwards Teapot.

THE DRAG

This is a pretty movement in which you skate forward on one foot, then bend your skating knee fully, but keep your body perfectly erect and square to the tracing. At the same time, swing your free leg back and place the inside of your skating foot on the rink and drag it behind you (photographs 102, 103). This is a nice movement particularly for pair skaters, but, a word of caution – it can put undue wear on the side of your boot, so it must not be done too frequently. White boots are particularly prone to suffer in this way.

103. Side shot of the Drag.   104. Inside Spread Eagle.

THE SPREAD EAGLE

This is a movement in which both feet are on the rink at the same time, with the heels inwards and the toes turned away from each other. You should stand perfectly erect with your legs fully extended with straight knees. The inside Spread Eagle, (photograph 104) skated on inside edges, is the easiest of the movements, but the Spread Eagle may be skated on an outside edge, requiring more courage, or in a straight line. Make sure that your bottom is not sticking out when you do this and that your head is carried high.

These three free skating movements should be practised on both feet. They can be used to link other steps together, and even to commence or finish any programme.

One compulsory figure which can be introduced into free skating is the use of the change of edge. Whether skated to lead into a turn or jump, or used in spiral form to cover the whole rink, the change edge is an attractive movement to watch and is, moreover, one of the figures which a skater can really 'feel' when performing. The actual feel of a change of edge at high speed in an arabesque cannot properly be described – it has to be experienced – but it epitomises the freedom of skating in a personal way.

FREE SKATING PROGRAMMES

I think that the real joy and fun of skating lies in free skating executed as a programme. One can either piece together various steps and movements to skate to music on an ad lib basis, enjoying the music and letting it lead you from movement to movement or one can carefully work out a programme to selected music, so that they become a harmonious whole.

When I refer to free skating I am also including pair skating and free dancing within the term, though this is not strictly correct. It is great fun to vary dance steps to suit music, and even pair skating can be done on an ad hoc basis.

Once you can *skate* edges, do simple jumps and spins, and perform simple linking steps and dance steps, *in good form*, a free skating programme becomes possible. Free skating is not only good fun for the skater, if the movements are executed surely and in good style, however simple, but it also provides pleasure for spectators.

Initially the coach prepares the first free skating programme for a pupil, to show how to place the movements on the ice, how to spread out and balance the various elements, and how to select and skate to music. After that, however, you should not rely solely upon your teacher: you must use your own imagination to make up the programme, but always be ready to accept or seek guidance on technical matters, on presentation, and on matters which require experience. In fact, the budding free skater must learn to be his or her own choreographer!

105-107. The skater is executing a forward pivot on a right inside edge: her left toe is placed on the ice whilst she traces a circle round it.

Many clubs and associations hold primary competitions for novices and young skaters, and quite often the free skating competitions are limited to a jump, a spiral and a spin, and a programme length not exceeding $1\frac{1}{2}$ minutes duration. It is customary, too, in such competitions for only the very simple jumps and spins to be performed or allowed, and advanced steps, jumps, etc. are excluded, and can even penalize the skater!

The first step is to consider what you *can* do. Never try to include in a programme any movement or turn in which you are not proficient and confident. Having decided the movements you wish to use, the worst thing is to go out on the ice and try to put these into a programme immediately! Skate the movements individually. Try to skate at the speed you will be skating in the competition or exhibition and ascertain just how much surface each movement will cover. Having selected your music, which should not be too hackneyed or too trendy, skate some of your movements to the music and find out how many bars each move takes. Then get off the ice and start on the clerical work!

Make a map of the rink, marking on the centre line and transverse axes (as in the dance diagram layout), and place the movements on paper where you think they will take place. In this way it becomes easy to visualize the presentation and to plan the movements so that there is a balance. One cannot see oneself skating, unless a video-tape or ciné film is made, or a large mirror available.

108-110. A back pivot: (108) skating a back outside edge and about to bring the free foot across the line of skating; (109) dropping the toe on to the ice behind and across the skating leg and (110) skating a back outside edge by tracing a circle round the pivot toe.

Remember, you must not skate in one direction round the rink all the time, or place jumps and spins in a far corner. Nor should you execute all your best jumps and spins all together. Try to remember that in a competition the judges will be placed along one side of the rink and that, if you skate intricate or spectacular movements close to the judges' side and in a corner at the same time, it is hardly likely that they will be able to see them properly or mark them to greatest advantage. Try to place your spins along the centre line of the rink, and your best jumps across the centre spot. Above all, there must be continuous practice and rehearsal, until the whole programme becomes automatic and yet still looks alive and spontaneous. Should you fall or stumble, you can then get up and carry on skating as if nothing had happened. There is nothing worse than a slight fault which ends in a skater wandering about the rink trying to remember what step to do next and suffering from a brief loss of memory.

Start nicely, to attract attention, and then gradually skate with a continually improving programme until your best and most spectacular movements enable you to finish in such a way that judges and spectators would like to see more, and even feel that the programme was short. A boring, inefficient skater can make a two-minute programme seem like half an hour to the audience.

Before starting a programme, it is customary to have what is termed a warming up period on the ice, to skate around, loosen your muscles, and relax a little. Don't overdo this. Practise a few simple movements, get used to the ice, and quit before you either get tired or find yourself missing a difficult movement. Let the other competitors or exhibitors do that – it is the easiest thing in the world to leave the winner's place on the warming-up ice.

No matter how many times a skater performs or skates in a competition, the period before skating out on the ice is one when nerves are going to be tested. Your stomach will feel queer, your throat and mouth dry . . . but, the moment you skate out to take up your starting pose and the familiar music commences, all your nervousness will vanish and you will be able to concentrate on the task in hand.

10. Outdoor Ice Skating

Outdoor ice skating falls into two types: artificial rinks out-of-doors and natural ice formations. The latter includes lakes, reservoirs, ponds, rivers, canals and so on. The former category consists of proper outdoor rinks (sometimes with refrigerating equipment as in indoor rinks) and artificial rinks caused by the temporary flooding of fields, arenas etc. specifically for skating.

Outdoor skating, especially over natural ice, is a wonderful sport, particularly when one skates a long distance on canals or frozen rivers, or over large lakes. The air is clean, fresh and invigorating, and the ice surface, when at its best, 'sings' as one swoops along. On the other hand, skating, figures in particular, on an outdoor rink or over a frozen pond can pose problems. Firstly, there is the wind to consider: going one way round a figure can be fine, but the return journey against the wind, or with the wind, can wreck a tracing completely. Secondly, the ice surface can vary. On an indoor rink the ice is resurfaced between sessions, and on artificial outdoor rinks, this, too, is carried out, but over ponds and lakes the surface will vary according to the freezing conditions. The ice may be corrugated from wind action, branches or flotsam may be frozen into the surface to bring hazards to the skater, whilst the quality of the ice may vary. This can bring dangers if one should meet patches of thin or rotten ice, especially at the beginning of a freeze-up or after a thaw has started. Good outdoor ice is superb, however. It is even better than the artificial variety, and skating over this ice is the most exhilarating and thrilling experience for any ice skater!

Large expanses of ice which have only a few inches of water beneath or which is very thick due to an extreme climate are probably quite safe for racing and speed events, ice hockey and general skating. Cracks in the ice do not necessarily mean that it is dangerous, though a covering of an inch or so of snow may be: you may hit unseen obstacles such as sticks or stones, or run on to dangerous ice.

Clear black or green ice is stronger than white ice or snow ice. In general, for safety's sake, a minimum of two inches of black ice or five inches of snow ice is recommended. Always remember that for any type of ice its thickness is no real gauge of its safety.

Do *not* use your best skates for outdoor work over natural ice. The different conditions – hard and soft ice, corrugations or material frozen into the surface – can soon take the edge off your skates. It is best, too, to take the toe-picks from the front or grind them down, so that the rounded front of your skate will ride over obstacles instead of bringing you down. A typical hazard occurs when ice cracks and one piece rides higher than the other, and then freezes. The step thus formed, even if it is a small one, can cause a nasty tumble.

Remember, too, to wear warm clothes and take some extra ones to put on when you stop skating. If you are skating school figures you may well need to wear a pair of gloves. You should also take some extra clothes just in case you go through the ice.

If you fall through ice into deep water, you will be in very real danger of drowning, let alone freezing to death. If you go through when you are travelling at speed, you will be thrown forward, away from the hole, under the ice. Assuming that the shock of icy water does not immobilize you and that you can swim, you must try to find the hole that you made, which from under the surface shows up as a light patch against the dark ice.

If you see someone else go through the ice, try to find a long pole or rope to help him or her out, and do not let too many other people go near the hole. When the ice is quite thin and the water fairly shallow, say only a couple of feet, there is less difficulty, providing of course that it is not a small child who has fallen through: you can usually break a way through the ice to give assistance.

The wisest thing to do, if you are going to skate on natural ice, is to learn first of all how to swim. This may not only save your own life but might also prevent someone else losing his life trying to save you; you may, in addition, be called upon to save a friend.

Skating outdoors on natural ice is where the sport began; its magic is still strong and, no doubt, always will be.

11. Now You Can Ice Skate . . .

Once a skater has become fairly proficient at moving about in different steps and simple dances, the confines of the public session tend to become irksome: more space is needed, skaters of all degrees of proficiency are struggling to get a fair share of the rink, and it is difficult trying to practise. True, there are the dance intervals during which you may try your skill with either a professional or an amateur partner, but these do not satisfy the needs of the figure and free skater.

The solution lies, in many instances, in club facilities. Most rinks have an amateur skating club attached, affiliated to the national organization, where there are sessions for learning steps and dances, and where junior club, inter-club, and senior competitions are held. Such clubs are always ready to welcome the keen skater, but not so willing to welcome older social skaters. Clubs, too, generally require the candidate for membership to be able to skate some form of entrance test. Clubs do bring skaters together and provide a rare opportunity for the champion to skate with the learner. Some clubs unfortunately are beset by a 'win at all costs' attitude and certain of their members, instead of helping the less proficient, are merely there to use the club sessions as practice sessions and to collect all the trophies they can. A good club, on the other hand, will provide invaluable help.

It is absolutely essential for the beginner to have professional coaching as soon as possible. This book is intended to put the skater on the right lines and help him or her to skate properly, but private professional tuition is essential if progress is to be maintained. Select your instructor – for the male dancer a female teacher and a male teacher for the female pupil does make it

111-114. How movements can be incorporated into a free skating programme. Skated by the lovely Linda Davis, well-known professional show skater, the movements are from an inside Spread Eagle on to an inside backward pivot and culminating in a pose on both toe-picks.

easier. *For pairs, a good teacher is essential from the start.* For the figure skater, use of the rink between sessions, on what are termed 'patches', under the watchful eye of a coach is vital.

But, a word of caution: too many teachers are obsessed with getting as many pupils as possible to pass proficiency tests. This is good for national associations, as test fees are their life blood, but, in the end, this means the loss of many keen skaters annually. Though the number of skaters is enormous, the number who actually take proficiency tests and become members of national associations is quite small, and expands at an extremely slow rate. So, try to find an instructor who will encourage you to learn new movements, as well as one who will give you a sound basic training.

For the skater who wants to win titles, it is a long hard slog. You need endless practice time. Your skating is going to cost a great deal of money and you are going to have to eat, sleep and drink skating and skating techniques for 25 hours out of every 24! It is a sad and indisputable fact that an amateur devotes most of his or her time to practising and quite often, for years, has no regular or full-time employment whilst learning and practising. Indeed, the top amateur skaters of today are dedicated individuals who know little of anything else and are virtually 'professionals' insofar as skating time and opportunity are concerned.

Skating proficiency tests, though they are introduced with a view to encouraging the newcomer and to increasing the efficiency of techniques, unfortunately become harder each season. The standard gradually rises: one has only to see youngsters today quickly picking up techniques such as double jumps which a few years ago was unheard of. So, as you become more proficient, we ask you to give a helping hand to other, less competent skaters. Skate dances with a youngster or an older enthusiast and do not be afraid to give a helping hand (providing the professional coach who might be involved does not object). Be prepared to join in activities which will improve not only your own skating, but those of other people. Today there is unfortunately a sort of 'hate-the-Hun' attitude in certain competitive quarters – please do not indulge in this. Skating gives you an opportunity to enjoy your sport with your family, with friends, with old and young enthusiasts, with people of other nationalities and from other clubs.

If you aim to take proficiency tests, work hard at them and try to be a credit to your coach. Attend the test properly and neatly dressed, having checked your skates some days beforehand, with clean skating boots, and with a ready, cheerful smile. If the judges' decision goes against you, try to be cheerful about it and do not mutter about 'unfair judges', 'poor skating surface', 'bad music', 'rotten partner', 'poor coach' or whatever other comments one has heard skaters make in the past. You are not perfect and, though you and your coach may have felt you deserved to pass, the judges probably saw something your coach had missed or mistakes you made in the stress of the test.

Ice skating is a terrific sport, it is artistic and it can open horizons to you for years to come. Skaters who give up the sport generally return to it in later years, and some go on until they are well and truly in the octogenarian class! So, on with your ice skates and get out on to that ice to glide, spin, jump, dance, swerve and swoop!

A Note to Parents

Parents who have read this book should beware of the terrible label of 'skating parent' bestowed on certain individuals by professional coaches, judges and rink managements. Please do not interfere in any way with the coaching of your youngster, do not dispute the judges' decisions and do not criticize other skaters, trainers or competitors. You will only inculcate a prejudice against your own youngster. In other words: encourage, pay up and keep quiet!

It is generally the non-skating parent who is at fault, so, if you don't skate, get your boots and skates on and have a go! At least you'll be able to appreciate your youngster's problems . . . and you'll stop pushing him or her.